# UNDERSTANDING
# GLORIA NAYLOR

Understanding Contemporary American Literature
Matthew J. Bruccoli, Series Editor

**Volumes on**

Edward Albee • John Barth • Donald Barthelme • The Beats
The Black Mountain Poets • Robert Bly • Raymond Carver
Chicano Literature • Contemporary American Drama
Contemporary American Horror Fiction
Contemporary American Literary Theory
Contemporary American Science Fiction • James Dickey
E. L. Doctorow • John Gardner • George Garrett • John Hawkes
Joseph Heller • John Irving • Randall Jarrell • William Kennedy
Ursula K. Le Guin • Denise Levertov • Bernard Malamud
Carson McCullers • W. S. Merwin • Arthur Miller
Toni Morrison's Fiction • Vladimir Nabokov • Gloria Naylor
Joyce Carol Oates • Tim O'Brien • Flannery O'Connor
Cynthia Ozick • Walker Percy • Katherine Anne Porter
Reynolds Price • Thomas Pynchon • Theodore Roethke • Philip Roth
Hubert Selby, Jr. • Mary Lee Settle • Isaac Bashevis Singer
Jane Smiley • Gary Snyder • William Stafford • Anne Tyler
Kurt Vonnegut • Tennessee Williams • August Wilson

# UNDERSTANDING
# GLORIA
# NAYLOR

Margaret Earley Whitt

University of South Carolina Press

© 1999 University of South Carolina

Published in Columbia, South Carolina, by the
University of South Carolina Press

Manufactured in the United States of America

03  02  01  00  99     5  4  3  2  1

**Library of Congress Cataloging-in-Publication data**

Whitt, Margaret Earley, 1946–
        Understanding Gloria Naylor / Margaret Earley Whitt.
            p. cm.—(Understanding contemporary American literature)
        Includes bibliographical references (p. ) and index.

        ISBN 1-57003-273-4
        1. Naylor, Gloria—Criticism and interpretation. 2. Women
and literature—United States—History—20th century. 3. Afro-
American women in literature. 4. Afro-Americans in literature.
I. Title. II. Series.
PS3564.A895 Z96 1999
813'.54—dc21                                     98-40209

*For Ruth Meriwether Earley*

*And her great-grandchildren after her:*
*Thomas, Carson, Avery*

*and for*
*Charley and Jessica*
*and*
*Wintry*

# CONTENTS

# SERIES EDITOR'S PREFACE

The volumes of *Understanding Contemporary American Literature* have been planned as guides or companions for students as well as good nonacademic readers. The editor and publisher perceive a need for these volumes because much of the influential contemporary literature makes special demands. Uninitiated readers encounter difficulty in approaching works that depart from the traditional forms and techniques of prose and poetry. Literature relies on conventions, but the conventions keep evolving; new writers form their own conventions—which in time may become familiar. Put simply, *UCAL* provides instruction in how to read certain contemporary writers—identifying and explicating their material, themes, use of language, point of view, structures, symbolism, and responses to experience.

The word *understanding* in the titles was deliberately chosen. Many willing readers lack an adequate understanding of how contemporary literature works; that is, what the author is attempting to express and the means by which it is conveyed. Although the criticism and analysis in the series have been aimed at a level of general accessibility, these introductory volumes are meant to be applied in conjunction with the works they cover. They do not provide a substitute for the works and authors they introduce, but rather prepare the reader for more profitable literary experiences.

M. J. B.

# ACKNOWLEDGMENTS

My many thanks go to the following people who made their time available to me: first, Gloria Naylor, whose generous gift of time and hospitality on a July day in 1996 helped me to understand my own work more clearly and, more importantly, gave me a sense of her presence as a writer in the year that followed.

Peggy Keeran of Penrose Library at the University of Denver, Carol Taylor in the University Computing Lab, and Helene Orr of the English Department all provided necessary support when it mattered most. Jane Smith patiently read the manuscript chapter by chapter and gave good advice.

Others who entered into the discussion of the writing of Gloria Naylor with me and from whose viewpoints I was able to enlarge my own include my colleagues Barbara Wilcots, M. E. Warlick, Abbey Kapelovitz, Paula Sperry, Sarah Gordon, Eleanor McNees, Beth Nugent, Diana Wilson, Carol Samson, Judy Goldberg, Kathleen Barr, Sally Kurtzman, Dodi Vaughn, Gail Brown, Mary Metzger, Nan Holt, and Barb Stude.

Those who participated at the table discussion at the North Carolina lake house included Anne and T. G. Daniel, Karen and Mack Gaddy, Frankie and Roger Tipton, Katherine and Bob Moore. Those who listened in Florida—Marilyn and Ralph Heim, Sandra and Chad Adams—gave ongoing support. In South Carolina, Jackie and Dave Palmer opened their home to me on many occasions throughout the year and were always willing to hear my latest thoughts. My Texas connection—Pat Saxon—was essential to the progress of my work.

## ACKNOWLEDGMENTS

I am grateful to my students, who have shared with me the wisdom and delight in each of Naylor's novels and helped me to see more deeply, and especially to Danielle Roten who made a tape of the music Laurel Dumont listened to before she took her final dive. To those graduate students who came into the office and patiently listened to paragraphs-in-progress, my thanks—Jon Pinnow, Lisa Metzger, Nancy Hightower, Stuart Mills, Cynthia Kuhn, Ellen Melko, Christine Hume, Janet Bland, Kira Stevens, Catherine Kasper, Rich Caccavale, Jason Miller Caccavale, to name a few.

# UNDERSTANDING
# GLORIA NAYLOR

# CHAPTER ONE

# Understanding Gloria Naylor

## Career

Gloria Naylor's first four novels—*The Women of Brewster Place* (1982), *Linden Hills* (1985), *Mama Day* (1988), and *Bailey's Café* (1992)—constitute her quartet of novels, the books she planned as the foundation of her career.[1] Each of the novels in turn connects with the one to follow; mention of a character or a place in one becomes the central focus of the next. In the ten years that separate the first and fourth novel, Naylor demonstrates an increased sophistication in recasting character and place. In these novels children die, dreams get deferred, and place, whether literal or mythical, becomes a way station in life's journey. In each novel, a community of women emerges—sustaining, enabling, and enriching the lives of one another.

In the late 1970s, in a creative writing class at Brooklyn College, the professor told her students to be bold, send out their creative endeavors, and say that the sample was part of a larger work.[2] Gloria Naylor, sitting in that class, took this advice and mailed off "A Life on Beekman Place" to *Essence*. They published the story in March 1980 while Naylor was still an undergraduate; it was an early draft of the "Lucielia Louise Turner" chapter/story in the work-in-progress that was to become her first novel.

In 1982 *The Women of Brewster Place: A Novel in Seven Stories* was published by Viking Press. Describing the female residents in looks and lifestyles was important to Naylor. As she states in a 1989 interview in *Ebony,* "One character couldn't be *the* Black woman in America. So I had seven different women, all in different circumstances, encompassing the complexity of our lives, the richness of our diversity, from skin color on down to religious, political and sexual preferences."[3] The following year the novel won the American Book Award for Best First Novel. From the beginning, reviewers looked at Naylor's work alongside that of Toni Morrison and Alice Walker, who published *The Color Purple* the same year. Naylor, who had herself only recently discovered the existence of a long black literary tradition, was suddenly a part of it. When *Ebony* touted the reigning black women novelists in 1984, Naylor was the chosen representative of those who "are coming forward to take their place in the sun."[4]

Her second novel, *Linden Hills,* was published by Ticknor & Fields in 1985. At Brooklyn College, Naylor had been reading Dante's *Inferno* in a survey course of great works of western literature when it occurred to her that Dante's structure would work for the neighborhood she had in mind, a place where its inhabitants sell their souls for a piece of the American Dream—a home in the right neighborhood, a marriage partner to enhance an image, and children who would carry on the design. To be successful in Linden Hills meant obtaining an address as close as possible to the lowest circle of this upscale hell.

Three years later, in 1988, Ticknor & Fields published *Mama Day.* From three perspectives, Naylor delivers the love story of George and Cocoa—from the points of view of George, Cocoa, and the mystical island of Willow Springs, an island off the coast of Georgia and South Carolina, which speaks for itself and does not appear on any map. The reader's attention and consciousness must shift from New York City to Willow Springs, from the world of rational, logical thought to a place of otherworldliness, where "across the bridge" thinking does not make sense on an island imbued with the haunting power of Miranda (Mama) Day. This is a large novel in every aspect, one in which Naylor demonstrates that love's power operates in ways the human mind can only begin to fathom. References to Shakespeare abound in this novel and are most apparent in her use of *The Tempest.*

The way in which life operates on Willow Springs moves this novel into the mythic realm. Suspending belief is paramount to accepting, if not completely understanding, Willow Springs and the conjuring activities of Mama Day. Listening is important in any Naylor novel, and in *Mama Day* the author gives instructions on how to listen. The reader needs to understand that words will appear which no one speaks, unknown words will have a variety of meanings depending on context, and known words may mean something other than what the reader thinks. A story exists below the surface of the words; to read the story thoughtfully is to listen actively to a world that makes its own sense.

Similar instruction is given at the beginning of Naylor's 1992 *Bailey's Café* when the reader discovers that words are symbols for music: "There's a whole set to be played here if you want to stick around and listen to the music."[5] The culminating novel of the quartet, which has also been rewritten and presented as a play, is organized around a jazz set. All the world's a jam, it would seem, and its players merely instruments upon the stage. As in the beginning of Naylor's career, the seven "women" of Brewster Place are now a new seven women who wander into the world of the maestro, a man often called Bailey, who happened to buy a café by that name and never bothers to tell its visitors that Bailey is not his name. The café is introduced in *Mama Day,* but when it appears in the fourth novel, it is no longer in one specific place; it may exist anywhere. People who need it will always be able to find it. Life has not been kind to the characters assembled here, but their stories, which reflect who these women are, like everything that matters in life, are below the surface (19).

In *The Men of Brewster Place,* her 1998 fifth novel published by Hyperion, Naylor returns to familiar territory. While Brewster Place's women take center stage in her first novel, Naylor shifts her focus to the men that add meaning to the lives of their women. The flat single roles the men played in the first novel are expanded here, giving depth and understanding to their personalities. Man by man, their individual relationships with the women are placed in larger contexts. While no community of men emerges, Naylor ends this novel with hope.

Naylor's writing includes other genres. She has written personal essays for *Essence, Life, People,* and the *New York Times* and its magazine. She has edited and written an introduction for *Children of the Night: The Best Short Stories by Black Writers, 1967 to the Present.*

## Overview

Down deep, there is something inherently southern in Gloria Naylor. It can be seen in the way she tells a story, paying careful attention to the details of her characters' lives, and in the painstaking meticulousness with which she draws the places where those fictional characters dwell. Though she was born in New York City, she was conceived in Robinsonville, Mississippi, the oldest daughter of sharecropping parents who had spent their days in Tunica County in the Mississippi Delta, in the northwest corner of this cotton-growing state. Roosevelt and Alberta McAlpin Naylor left Mississippi in December 1949 so that their first child could be born in the North, a part of the country that her parents perceived would offer educational opportunities for this unborn child and those that would follow. Her mother loved to read but was denied the use of the public library because of her skin color. It was coming North that provided her parents with the opportunity to become real Americans and to see their children spend their youth dealing "*within* this society,"[6] for at mid-century, Mississippi was very much a closed society, as historian James Silver called it, to those other than white Christians.[7]

Naylor has said that it was her "conception in the South that has played the more important role in shaping [her] life as a writer."[8] She was born on January 25, 1950, a birthday she shares with Virginia Woolf, who once asked a question which Naylor appears to answer in her writing: "Why are women . . . so much more interesting to men than men are to women?"[9] Naylor's response expands Woolf's statement, suggesting that women can also be more interesting to women.

Naylor was a high school senior honor student at Andrew Jackson High in Queens when Martin Luther King, Jr., was assassinated in April 1968. Naylor found her response to that event influenced by her mother's conversion to the Jehovah's Witnesses and that group's message of a theocratic government. At the time becoming a Jehovah's Witness missionary seemed appropriate, so she got behind the wheel of her Dodge Dart and took to "the dusty byroads leading from I-95 South, just wanting to see whatever the towns looked like wherever that road ended."[10] She was a missionary for seven years (1968–1975), spreading that message in New York; in and around Dunn, North Carolina; and in Jacksonville, Florida.

When she returned to New York, she enrolled in Medgar Evers College with plans to seek a degree in nursing. When the study of literature began to occupy more of her time, she transferred to Brooklyn College of the City University of New York and graduated with a B.A. in English in 1981. As Naylor relates in her 1985 "Conversation" with Toni Morrison, in her creative writing class she learned that in order to write good literature, one had to read good literature. The list included Tillie Olsen, Henry James, and Toni Morrison, but it was Morrison's *The Bluest Eye* that had a singular significance: "Time has been swallowed except for the moment I opened that novel because for my memory that semester is now *The Bluest Eye,* and *The Bluest Eye* is the beginning. The presence of the work served two vital purposes at that moment in my life. It said to a young poet, struggling to break into prose, that the barriers were flexible; at the core of it all is language, and if you're skilled enough with that, you can create your own genre. And it said to a young black woman, struggling to find a mirror of her worth in this society, not only is your story worth telling but it can be told in words so painstakingly eloquent that it becomes a song."[11]

A scholarship for graduate work at Yale made it possible for Naylor to pursue her newly discovered awareness of a long and rich black literary tradition. *Linden Hills,* her second novel, became the creative thesis for an M.A. in Afro-American Studies from Yale in 1983, a manuscript she completed while teaching at George Washington University. In 1985 Naylor won a National Endowment for the Arts fellowship and served as a cultural exchange lecturer in India for the United States Office of Information. In 1986 she was visiting professor at New York University and wrote several HERS columns for the *New York Times* on such topics as psychics, dating, and the popularity of the television game show *Wheel of Fortune.* She also won the Candace Award of the National Coalition of One Hundred Black Women. In "Reflections," a piece in *Centennial,* she interviewed her parents, who had by this time been married thirty-six years, about their varying reasons for leaving the South and coming to New York.

Naylor was a visiting lecturer at Princeton in 1987 and a recipient of a Guggenheim Fellowship in 1988. Other universities at which she taught or lectured include the University of Pennsylvania, Boston University, Brandeis University, and Cornell University. She was a visiting scholar at the University of Kent in Canterbury, England, in 1992. From 1989 to 1994 she served on the Executive Board of the Book-of-the-Month Club. In order for Naylor to have control over her books as they move into various genres, she formed One Way Productions in 1990.

Naylor sees herself as a filter through which her characters come to life.[12] She has expressed disappointment, for example, that George in *Mama Day* turned out to be a football fan, which required of Naylor hours of research on a sport that did not interest her.[13] Also, she was not pleased that in *Linden Hills* Willa Prescott Nedeed came out of that basement with her dead child prepared to clean the house: "What that woman finally came to, after that whole travail, was that she was a good wife and a good mother and that she could go upstairs and claim that identity. That is not what I thought Willa would do, but Willa was Willa."[14] In what she calls her psychic revelations, her characters assert themselves, and she feels obliged to honor those images. Characters in a book not yet written appear to her, and it is only later that she knows what to do with them. As an example she tells this story: "One image that kept haunting me from even before I finished *Linden Hills:* a woman carrying a dead male baby through the woods to this old woman. I didn't know why she was carrying the dead baby, but I knew her name because the old lady said, 'Go home, Bernice. Go home and bury your child.'"[15] Several years later when she was working on *Mama Day,* it occurred to Naylor that Bernice's baby, the one she had gone to such extremes to conceive, was going to die. Naylor acknowledges that while she is not slave to those images, she does feel compelled to honor them.

Naylor conceived her quartet in the late 1970s, knowing that the composition could begin after she had her titles, dedications, and the last lines in mind. Writing about the black community in all its multivocality and displaying her characters in colors she describes as nutmeg, ebony, saffron, cinnamon red, gold, nut brown, smoky caramel, to list a few, were of paramount importance to her in a time when many black writers were expected to depict *the* black experience. Each of the four novels was to be a voice representing some part of the black community: *The Women of Brewster Place* was meant to "celebrate the female spirit and the ability to *transcend* and also to give a microcosm of Black women in America—Black women who are faced by a wall of racism and sexism."[16] In this quartet Naylor provides stories in octaves, themes in refrain, and characters in repetition. With the addition of her fifth novel, Naylor's pattern of character and geographical connection continues.

In *The Women of Brewster Place* Naylor uses the seven different notes of a musical scale to convey seven different stories. *Linden Hills* also has seven stories; the grace notes of shorter, quicker stories attached sound the various alarms—losses, one by one, of everything that was once held most dear: love, food, religion, music, athletic endeavor, family, and the connection with the past. As a celebration of love and magic, *Mama Day* explores a "brave new world that has such people in it," as Shakespeare reminds the reader in *The Tempest.* For here, characters who are dead talk without words to characters who are alive and listening. The romantic love story is embraced within a familial love that resonates with magic, orchestrated by Mama Day's hands that move to and with a tempo which she alone hears. In the final novel of the quartet, *Bailey's Café,* Naylor presents its seven stories of female sexuality through the blues, best delivered by jazz. Each character is a living embodiment of pain so deep that movement away from its source, a recurring motif in the blues, is an urgent necessity. The café as way station is all that is left in this world for a moment of rest. The black man's blues is the pulse of *The Men of Brewster Place,* and the novel's last line offers a possible prediction of Naylor's future direction: "the music plays on . . . and on . . ." (173).

# CHAPTER TWO

# *The Women of Brewster Place*

To date, *The Women of Brewster Place* has had two lives—one when the novel was published by Viking in 1982 and a second when the novel was produced as a made-for-television movie in 1989. With Oprah Winfrey as the executive producer and starring as Mattie Michael, this visual enactment of Naylor's work brought a second round of printed attention to the dead-end street where seven black women, having arrived through various routes and means, find themselves. For example, several months before the movie premiered in March of 1989, *Redbook* reprinted the Mattie Michael portion of the novel, with the title of "Mama Still Loves You."[1] In 1980 and 1982 *Essence* published two stories—an early draft, entitled "A Life on Beekman Place," of what would become the "Lucielia Louise Turner" chapter[2] and the Kiswana Browne story, published under the title, "When Mama Comes to Call. . . ."[3]

*Essence,* with a circulation of just under a million has, since its inception in 1970, been marketed to African-American women. It is ranked by *Magazines for Libraries* "among the top for readership among African-American adults" and is said to "appeal to both a male and a female audience."[4] On the other hand, *Redbook,* with a history dating back to 1903 and a circulation of some five million, appeals to "young married women and mothers" and its fiction is generally "romance or family oriented."[5] *Redbook*'s decision to publish Naylor's story in late 1988 recognized her writing as having audience appeal beyond the African-American community.

Contemporary reviewers welcomed the first life of *The Women of Brewster Place*, and, not unexpectedly, the strongest, most positive comments were from women who praised Naylor's representation of community. Dorothy Wickenden of the *New Republic* highlighted the desperate charms of the dead-end street, cast the men who visit at night as leaving behind "babies and bile," and favorably compared the novel to Alice Walker's *The Color Purple,* which was published the same year. Wickenden sensed the power that permeates the community as these women "through laughter and companionship . . . make themselves virtually impregnable."[6] Annie Gottlieb, writing for the *New York Times Book Review,* sees the female bonding that happens on Brewster Place as an example of a feminist issue that had been pressed by the "vanguard of the women's movement"—the need for women to pay attention to their relationships with other women. Historically, women have written about women in relationship with men. Now here was a book where "women are the foreground figures, primary both to the reader and to each other, regardless of whether they're involved with men." But Gottlieb does not let the issue rest, choosing to see the novel not as realistic but rather as mythic. The characters, though vivid and earthy, "seem constantly on the verge of breaking out into magical powers."[7]

On the other hand, Loyle Hairston, writing for *Freedomways,* a quarterly review of the Freedom Movement, points out Naylor's shortcomings in addressing the issues of the Movement. Hairston chastises her for not being more politically correct, calling her a "kind of closet social Darwinist who does not see the U.S. as oppressive." He claims that the narrative "gives no hint that its author is in serious conflict with fundamental U.S. values." Hairston overlooks, marginalizes, and minimizes the supportive female community precisely because Naylor "bypasses provocative social themes to play, instead, in the shallower waters of isolated personal relationships."[8] Hairston acknowledges Naylor's entry in the literary world as an enjoyable read, but hopes that her "next offering will plumb further the depths of human experience."[9]

Naylor opens her novel with an epigraph—Langston Hughes' poem "Harlem," which appeared as part of his 1951 collection *Montage of a Dream Deferred.* In writing about this collection, Hughes commented as though all the poems were part of a whole and related them in their entirety to "Afro-American popular music and the sources from which it has progressed—jazz, ragtime, swing, blues, boogie-woogie, and be-bop." Naylor's vision is reflected in Hughes' words on the collection of his poems: "This poem on contemporary Harlem, like be-bop, is marked by conflicting changes, sudden nuances, sharp and impudent interjections, broken rhythms, and passages sometimes in the manner of the jam session, sometimes the popular song, punctuated by the riffs, runs, breaks, and distortions of the music of a community in transition."[10]

"Harlem," like the novel, is about the possible consequences of dreams deferred; it presents seven questions or situations which parallel the circumstances of the seven women of Brewster Place and their respective stories. The poem does not provide answers, but the way in which the poet asks questions suggests that the answers are all in the affirmative: Dreams dry up like raisins in the sun, fester and run like sores, stink like rotten meat, crust and sugar over like syrupy sweets, sag like a heavy load, and finally explode—just as the collective women of Brewster Place do at novel's end in Mattie's dream, when together they tear down the wall, once baptized by vomit and later stained by blood. According to critic James Emanuel, the poem "traces in figurative language the long scar of psychic abuse which might . . . develop a fatally eruptive itch."[11] His suggestion of an eruptive itch falls far short of the power that deferred dreams have in *The Women of Brewster Place*.

The book is framed by a mythical, metaphorical day—"Dawn" to "Dusk"—in which the street comes to life through an ugly birthing process and at novel's end waits to die.[12] Brewster Place is located in a poor section of a large unnamed city, akin to New York City. Its origins are bleak: it is a bastard child, created by the wiles of men in clandestine meetings, not with the hope of new life entering prime real estate, but rather with the aim of economic gratification, individual mercenary urges pulsing toward the "consummation" of their respective desires (1). These ravenous men will "erect" and then "abate," all in the proverbial damp, smoke-filled room, so that Brewster Place can be "conceived" (1). Naylor's word choice is overtly sexual and deliberately skewed.

From the first paragraph the reader knows that the origins of Brewster Place are foreboding. Its birth comes three months after the conception, and, as could have been predicted by such beginnings, its true parentage is hidden (1). Given time, origins cease to matter and a community can forget, so by the time the baptism occurs two years later and a representative of the legislature breaks a bottle of champagne against a corner of one of the buildings, people can cheer (1). In a city that is growing and prospering, Brewster Place had a possibility of becoming "part of the main artery of the town" (2). As blood flows through human arteries from the heart to the various organs and parts of the body, vital to sustaining life and activity, Brewster Place as artery suggests the only glimmer of hope for this malconceived offspring of greed. But when representatives of power in the legislature fight for their own various small veins as though they know the lifeblood of their community depends on it, Brewster Place experiences the effects of racism in the American city. Brewster Place was never home to the dominant white society; it was home instead to "dark haired and mellow-skinned Mediterraneans," who carried the cultural marks of their ethnicity with them in their sounds and smells (2). There was no spokesperson who mattered, who would be listened to, to sustain Brewster Place as artery. In other words, no white person cared enough. When a wall was erected, making Brewster Place a literal dead-end street, it had the effect of a huge clamp, clotting the blood flow that could have kept it vibrantly alive.

In 1953, in the fictional world of Brewster Place, a brown-skinned man known as Ben came to integrate this Mediterranean world. As handyman/janitor who would do the work that the tenants would never consider doing, Ben is always "less than." He uses the polite deference of "yessem" to the paler Europeans; he is a harmless "nice colored man," as though the adjective colored necessitated specific and hasty categorizing. He could be courted by lonely women with homemade soup and bread, but, instinctively, taught by a lifetime of being

reminded of his place because of his strange hair and skin, Ben
knew never to show up at someone's door without the tools of
his trade as his entry—a broom, a wrench (3). Naylor places
Ben in the foreground, creating around him a kind of mystery,
a story not yet told. Because Ben is the focus, Naylor makes
this marginalized character central and sympathetic.

The Mediterraneans had seen Brewster Place through both
its youth and middle age—the bastard child does grow up. In
its old age, after the erection of that wall and the exodus of one
group and the relocation of the colored daughters to the only
place left that would have them, Brewster Place experiences a
revitalization. Naylor's black women who come to Brewster
Place are experiencing hard times, and their life choices, for
whatever reasons, have been reduced. But Naylor makes clear
in the "Dawn" of this day, at the beginning of the book, that
these women, though down, are by no means out. Naylor uses
repeated images of strength and laughter to counter what could
be a prevailing notion: a person down on her luck would be
despondent.

Naylor creates a sassiness in her women who claim their
space in Brewster Place with an assurance that does not depend
on male approval, that functions confidently on its own terms:
"straight-backed, round-bellied, high-behinded women who
threw their heads back when they laughed and exposed strong
teeth and dark gums" (4–5). These women are prepared to help
one another. Naylor draws on a final image of an ebony
phoenix to conclude "Dawn." The classical myth of the
phoenix, with its many variations, has to do with a fabulous
bird, resembling an eagle, that every five hundred years burns
itself on a funeral pyre and out of its decomposing body rises

again. These women will not disappear, grow old and die. For through their stories, "each in her own time and with her own season" will rise again (5). The image of these women as a collective phoenix testifies to their indestructibility.

After the seven stories of these women are told, "The Block Party" attempts to draw the community together—and does so in two entirely separate ways. Its function is also to bring to a close a literal day and turn that day into a metaphor: the book begins in "Dawn" and concludes in "Dusk." It is "Dusk," not only on this day, but on everything that Brewster Place has been. In "Dawn," when Brewster Place was conceived, it was humanized, but here at its death, it is dehumanized by Naylor's use of negative images to announce its death. Its conception is recast at the end, the story is rewritten; where earlier it had been "conceived," now it had been "spawned" (191). Besides being associated with the activity of aquatic animals producing numerous offspring, the use of "spawn" is often contemptuous. All the people have abandoned Brewster Place, and the colored daughters, a reminder of what this book has been about, have taken their collective phoenix elsewhere, and those deferred dreams, the ones that eventually do explode on Brewster Place, are still dreams that will "ebb and flow, but never disappear" (192). Like the phoenix, these women will rise again. It is only the empty Brewster Place that can die, and, at novel's end, still waits to do so.

## "Mattie Michael"

As Naylor prepares the reader for the women's individual stories, she says that "each in her own time and with her own season" will rise again (5). For Mattie Michael, who serves this novel as matriarch, surrogate mother, and mentor to the other women on Brewster Place, the season is winter and the time is only a moment. For the reader to understand how Mattie, the proud mother of an only child named Basil, has lost her home, Naylor moves from the real time of a moment into memory, which recalls Mattie's story. To do so, Naylor uses tangible objects to mark the passing and collapsing of time, specifically the opening use of plants and later the use of oatmeal.

When Mattie first arrives on Brewster Place, it is a snowy day. By indirection Naylor lets the reader have hints of Mattie's past. Mattie comes, bearing beautiful plants, personified and central in the description, for it is the plants that are in the fore-ground; once they "had an entire sun porch for themselves in the home she had exchanged thirty years of her life to pay for" (7). Using the sense that is most often connected with memory, Naylor uses the smells of someone's cooking to take Mattie back in time, into her youth, so that her story can begin. The smell she inhales is "like freshly cut sugar cane" (8), and sugar cane leads directly to "summer and Papa and Basil and Butch" (8). How she comes to Brewster Place is not just background information, but essential to understanding the strength she will exhibit in her new surroundings.

All the pages that follow this moment are in the time of memory. Mattie, led by her sense of smell, moves through time that, as Naylor captures it, "is like molten glass that can be opaque or crystallize at any given moment at will: a thousand days are melted into one conversation, one glance, one hurt, and one hurt can be shattered and sprinkled over a thousand days" (35). When Mattie goes to sleep that first Saturday night in Eva Turner's home, she awakes Sunday morning, but memory time takes over the narrative—for years have passed—and Basil and Ciel, Miss Eva's granddaughter, are now rambunctious children. On this new morning, briefly in real time, Miss Eva prepares the oatmeal, but before the children can finish the meal, memory time returns. Basil's bowl of oatmeal, food that represents a source of strength and a means of keeping him alive, becomes a literal measure of his growth. In memory or collapsed time, the oatmeal causes Basil's legs to reach from the first rung to the second rung of his chair. But from one rung to the next, collapsing all the events that happen in real time, Miss Eva would be dead (40). And when Mattie looks at him again, once more in a shift to real time, Basil has become a man, "gulping coffee and shoveling oatmeal into his mouth" (41). It is still Sunday morning. Oatmeal serves not only as a literal meal at breakfast time, but also as a powerful and useful tool to manipulate time. Through Basil's eating oatmeal, Naylor moves the narrative from Basil's childhood to his adulthood.

Naylor's use of language, including her figures of speech, particularly unusual ones, are worth noting for how closely those choices respond to thematic development. Butch, Mattie's only-time lover and Basil's father, is cinnamon red (8), sparks of fire highlight his body (10), and in an excellent example of synesthesia, his laugh is like "the edges of an April sunset" (9). When Mattie agrees to go caning with him, the "April sun set in its full glory" (11). Naylor's use of each of these images continues to build on the blood-red imagery that she begins with in "Dawn." Butch's connection with Mattie follows his "sugar cane theory" of life: "Eating cane is like living life. You gotta know when to stop chewing—when to stop trying to wrench every last bit of sweetness out of a wedge—or you find yourself with a jawful of coarse straw that irritates your gums and the roof of your mouth" (18).

Seduced by his language, his looks, and her physical response to him, Mattie is a willing sex partner for Butch on this hot summer afternoon. Naylor describes the act of sex in detail, but she does it in Butch's mind. In reality, Mattie is talking and Butch is staring intently at her face, but in one of the longest sentences in the novel (86 words), that carries its own breathlessness down the page, "his mind slipped down the ebony neck that was just plump enough for a man to bury his nose into and suck up tiny bits of flesh that were almost as smooth as the skin on the top of her full round breasts that held nipples that were high, tilted, and unbelievably even darker than the breasts, so that when they touched the tongue there was the sensation of drinking rich, double cocoa" (17). By the end of the sentence, the reader forgets that all this is happening only in Butch's mind. The reality of the act itself does not take place in the language of the afternoon they spend together. The reader knows it happens, however, because in a few pages Mattie is pregnant. Where it must have happened has to be the "deep green basil and wild thyme [that] formed a fragrant blanket on the mossy earth" (15). When the baby is born, Mattie names him Basil, the site of his conception, locking in the memory of physical place. According to herbal lore, basil is used as a love charm and, in various legends, has some peculiar effect on women.[13]

In his afternoon with Mattie, Butch prepares the reader for Mattie's father before he is introduced in the text. Butch hints at incest: "What he savin' you up for—his self?" (13). Samuel Michael is an ambiguous character, stagnating in an Old Testament view of life. He makes enormous personal sacrifices for this daughter, "the only child of his autumn years" (19); he works overtime to buy her small luxuries, and places his concern for her health above responsibilities for his farm. Her pregnancy, however, closes him down, and two days of the silent treatment, while he stews in his chair with the Bible on his lap, torment Mattie. Naylor uses the silent treatment to parallel the uneasy calm before a storm. The storm itself takes place in the narrator's explosive language. Mattie is more frightened by the meaning of that silence than the physical violence which comes later. When Mattie refuses to identify the baby's father, Samuel's reaction to her words is out of proportion. First, Naylor's language creates a whirlwind, reminiscent in its power of the one that took Elijah up into heaven. Naylor's whirlwind "crumbled her father's face and exploded both of their hearts into uncountable pieces. She saw them both being spun around the room and sucked out of the windows along with everything that had ever passed between them" (22). The erupting figurative whirlwind becomes suddenly literal, as her father begins to slap her face, yank her hair, and beat her body with a broom. Only more violence, Mattie's mother's use of the shotgun, can snap him out of the trance; he sees what he has done and weeps.

Naylor uses the violence of the language to create a greater horror for the reader than the physical explosion. Mattie prefers and wishes for the physical violence over the hurt she feels from spoken words. When Basil is in jail, he lashes out at Mattie not in physical violence but in language that rips her to pieces: "There's nothing left to talk about, Mama, unless you wanna hear about the broken toilets with three-day-old shit or the bedbugs that have ate up my back or the greasy food I keep throwing up" (49). Mattie wishes he "had chosen a kinder way of hurting her, by just hitting her in the face" (49). For Mattie, physical violence is preferable because it is quicker and the pain is shorter. Language hangs in the mind, echoes in its recurring visits, causing the pain to repeat itself for years.

Naylor's word choices suggest an abstraction made concrete, and by inversion she heightens awareness of what is absent. Through language, Basil becomes a tangible part of Mattie, who lacks protected boundaries for herself: "She took in his happiness and made it her own just as she'd done with every emotion that had ever claimed him" (51). For thirty years of Basil's life she allows his feelings to dictate her own. During the last two weeks Basil spends with his mother, she becomes extra conscious of his presence. This awareness serves to highlight his absence. As at the police station when she cannot find him, it terrifies her (45). On the day Basil says good-bye to his mother in the morning, he is not there to pick her up in the afternoon. Acting unconsciously, in response to a subconscious dread, Mattie takes a bus home, stops by the store, enters the house through the back door, and remains in the kitchen. She does not want to face the stillness of the house nor see what she "would not" (53). Naylor inverts her language to call attention to negative space, which dwells on Mattie's response to Basil's departure, rather than to the overt action of Basil's leave taking. Mattie, had she gone in to the other rooms, would have seen a space where a jacket "would not be," a space where a portable radio "would not be," and spaces upstairs where suitcase and toothpaste "would not be" (53). Because Mattie chooses not to see what she "would not," Basil's absence takes on a weight that Mattie carries with her to Brewster Place.

Naylor's choices of particular details allude to places that exist and other African-American writers. Rockvale, which is located in Rutherford County near Nashville, Tennessee, produced sugar cane during the first half of the century on land owned by the Morgans, the name Naylor chooses to show ownership of the sugar cane fields by the levee where Butch is heading.[14] Her placement of Mattie in the rural environment of Rock Vale and the description of Mattie's response to Butch Fuller are strikingly similar to Janie Crawford's response to Johnny Taylor in Zora Neale Hurston's *Their Eyes Were Watching God*. Butch's "sugar cane theory" of life clearly echoes the same metaphor that, as Susan Meisenhelder has pointed out, Hurston exploits in her story, "Sweat."[15]

Mattie's love for her son is similar to what Toni Morrison will call "thick love"—the kind of love Sethe has for Beloved in *Beloved,* a novel published after *Women of Brewster Place;* the warnings which Miss Eva gives to Mattie over the years about Basil sound like Paul D's reminders to Sethe: "You your best thing, Sethe. You are."[16] Mattie cannot hear Miss Eva— not when she makes a suggestion about Basil's upbringing and not when she hints that Mattie's life needs someone else in it besides Basil.

Like the Papa Legba figure in African-American literature who meets characters at crossroads and leads them in the way they must go, Miss Eva's appearance and offer of a place to stay is precisely timed. Miss Eva sees the literal confusion of Mattie as she circles the block; however, Mattie has arrived at a figurative crossroad—she can go home to Rock Vale or keep searching for a rat-free environment in the city. The reference to going home is repeated a half dozen times; it remains the sole alternative to any of various hopes in the city for Mattie. What Miss Eva offers at this crossroad is a home and another chance to be successful in the city.

From the beginning Miss Eva's words issue a caution and forecast what Mattie comes to know too late: "Ya know, you can't keep him runnin' away from things that hurt him. Sometimes, you just gotta stay there and teach him how to go through the bad and good of whatever comes" (31). In recurring images, Miss Eva's eyes, which are faded blue, pitying, and freakish, find a way to move into Mattie's unconscious like a blue laser (38–39). When Eva is dead, Mattie knows too late that Eva has warned her of the day when Basil would separate himself from her and fill his life with choices that pleased only himself. His mother has taught him well by repeated examples of her over-indulgences on his behalf. Because she did not listen to Miss Eva, Mattie reaps severe consequences; she feels the hollowness and hunger of empty, unattended-to inside places. In fact, the Mattie-Basil relationship represents an extreme of black mother-to-son parenting often found in African-American literature: "mothers who love their sons to destruction through self-sacrifice and overindulgence"; Mattie serves as a "buffer between her son and the hostile world of both intra and interracial violence. . . . The result is a human being stripped of personhood, a man-child emasculated."[17]

*The Women of Brewster Place* is a tribute to a community of women of which Mattie is its hub. When she departs from Rock Vale, she begins her life-long commitment to a company of women. She seeks out first Etta Mae Johnson, an old friend from home, in some city along the Greyhound bus route. While Asheville, North Carolina, is mentioned as the first stop along the way, it is more likely that Etta Mae lives above the Mason-Dixon line. Etta Mae represents the best Mattie can do to replicate the familiarity of home, while Basil, who is yet to be, represents a literal taking of the past with her into a future that would be determined by the singular sexual action of her past.

The last section of "Mattie Michael" places the reader in real time, a short period before Mattie makes her appearance on Brewster Place. It is November, a reminder of the winter snow that Mattie stands in at the beginning of her story. Basil is in jail, and, expectedly, Mattie goes to his rescue. Because of Basil's exaggerated fear of a few more nights in jail, Mattie uses her home as security to obtain his bail money. Basil knows exactly how to work his mother, telling her he heard "rats under [his] bed last night" (48). His reference to rats is a fierce reminder of the rat she found biting his cheek as a baby. Because he leaves the city before his trial, Mattie loses her home of thirty years.

From the time when Mattie first notices the smell of some-one's cooking (8) to when the mover taps her on the shoulder (54), only a moment has passed. Everything necessary to know about Mattie's life before Brewster Place has been told. The reader has the information to use in the succeeding stories/chapters where Mattie's presence will continue to be felt. Mattie worries for her plants that she knows will die here on Brewster Place. She refuses to think consciously that she, too, will die here "because there just wasn't enough life left for her to do it all again" (7). The snowflake that rolls down her back like a frozen tear (54) as she unlocks the apartment for the movers, who think she may be a mental case, prepares the reader for the sadness that lies ahead.

## "Etta Mae Johnson"

Naylor moves the season and time from a winter moment to a summer day. Etta's return, her church attendance, her love-making with the preacher followed by his quick rejection of her all take place within a single day. The day represents a culmi-nating point in Etta's life, for in the years since she left Rock Vale, she had been trying to be herself in a place and time that saw only black and female. In Etta, Naylor presents a woman who struggles against prejudices, uses the music of Billie Hol-iday to deal with rejection, and finds temporary comfort in the sustaining friendship of Mattie within the community of Brewster Place.

Life has been hard for Etta. She was unwilling to play by the rules because "her spirit challenged the very right of the game to exist" (59). Part of the reason for Etta's peripatetic lifestyle was her search, not only for a man, but also for a place where she could be herself. Thinking that Rock Vale would be the only place where a black person would be expected to give a second thought to the slightest details of daily living, asking only that she be able to look a person in the face, smile when she pleased, and be polite when someone deserved it, she found that Rock Vale followed her to all the other cities. In 1937 "America wasn't ready for her yet" (60). Naylor's choice of date reflects a pre-World War II existence, when throughout the South, segregation was mandated by law. The specific initiative for Etta to leave Rock Vale is some unstated happening between herself and Johnny Brick. She had departed three hours ahead of his "furious pursuing relatives" and when she did not return, Brick's kin burned to the ground Etta's father's barn. While Etta wishes she had "killed the horny white bastard when she had the chance" (60), her father appears relieved that all he lost was the barn.

In these few lines, Naylor creates a familiar scenario; the understatement of the event heightens its injustice. The reference to "the horny white bastard" reflects a piece of the history of sexual practice in America. According to popular white opinion, "black women had strong passions and always desired sexual relations."[18] Especially in the South, where data indicate that literally millions of mixed-race children were born to black slave women, "both law and social thought encouraged white men to assume sexual access to female slaves."[19] History and habit of white entitlement led to a continuing of this attitude and the practice itself through the first half of the twentieth century.[20]

But what is it exactly that Etta did to Johnny Brick? Critic James Robert Saunders posits that "she retaliated violently to some kind of sexual indiscretion committed by Johnny" and that "what Johnny did was attempt to rape her."[21] What is just as likely to have happened is Etta's complete rejection of Johnny Brick's sexual advances, followed by lies on the part of Johnny to a confidant, who passes the word on to some appropriate person, creating "furious, pursuing relatives." Etta's father loses a barn and is told by the sheriff of Rutherford County, the one who has pledged to uphold and protect the rights of all people in the county, that he got off "mighty light." The sheriff's concern about Etta is nonexistent; the assumption of a white authority figure is that Etta got what she deserved because she must have asked for it, wanted it—in short, she did not remember her place in southern society. By agreeing with the sheriff, Mr. Johnson perpetuates southern racist behavior.

Naylor placed the text of the Lewis Allan song, "Strange Fruit," immediately preceding the paragraph explaining Etta's rapid departure from Rock Vale. This contrasts, on the one hand, the possibilities of death by lynching when a black male expresses interest in a white female and, on the other, the indifference southern society pays to a white male's carnal pursuit of a black female. "Strange Fruit" is a euphemism for "Black bodies swinging / In the Southern breeze."

Naylor begins the Etta Mae chapter/story with a description of an unidentified singer, one who fits the description of an aging Billie Holiday. The plumpness and white gardenias on the side of her head—a Holiday trademark—both hint at this possibility. Naylor describes the room as being taken "by its throat until it gasped for air" (55), something that only Billie was powerful enough to do. Naylor attributes the gasping to pain. "Billie's Blues," which a young Etta hears that night and never forgets, was to become one of Holiday's all-time classics, a familiar song she often began with, almost guaranteed to elicit "a huge roar of recognition from the crowd."[22] The selection and placement of Holiday's songs within the text is a commentary on Etta's story.

Etta returns to Brewster Place in a vinyl-topped Cadillac after a fling with a man wealthy enough to have owned it. Etta has done the best she could to prepare for her re-entry to the neighborhood—the car was clean and so were her clothes. She had changed her clothes ten minutes before arriving, no doubt in the restroom at the Mobil station where she had the car washed, and applied fresh make-up, which she then covered with large two-toned sunglasses (56). The Billie Holiday albums served as the cardboard armor (57) that helped her move past the staring neighbors who refused to call her by her first name. Her return was a story they already knew.

Etta's answer to those people is Holiday's song, "Tain't Nobody's Business if I Do." Because Holiday continued to sing this song through the years, she became identified with it. The young woman who sang with full understanding of the passion of young love became the older woman, who like Etta, lost her race with time as youth "gave way to a melancholy spirit trapped within the infinite loops of alcohol and drug addiction."[23] From Etta's perspective, Holiday's 1949 recording which projects the sassiness of spirit is her defense, but Naylor's placement also suggests how that same song for the neighbors came to represent Etta's own second place finish to time.

When Etta is safely harbored in Mattie's presence, the years of history between them permit the freedom of acceptance and laughter. As Etta tells Mattie the story of Simeon's Cadillac and displays the pink and red monogrammed shorts (58), Naylor interlaces the moment with Holiday's "God Bless the Child." The verse that is missing from the text identifies clearly what "his own" is: "Money, you got lots o' friends, / Crowd-in' 'round the door, / When you're gone and spend-in ends— / They don't come no more."[24] The song suggests that Simeon has some tough explaining to do to his wife, and without that Cadillac, he will be far less interesting to women he may have otherwise seduced. Simeon does not have "his own" anymore and "them that's not, shall lose" (59). Like the biblical Simeon (Genesis 42:24), this modern one is also held hostage. The last Holiday song included in the story is "Detour Ahead." The verse sums up the smooth beginning of the mating dance (70) Reverend Moreland Woods performs for Etta. As the couple glides away in his clean car with tinted windows, the song proclaims the wonder of love's simplicity, but ends with a hesitancy, asking "Can there be a detour ahead?" (71).

Mattie is a member of the Canaan Baptist Church, a place where its members "still worshipped God loudly" (62), a rich fertile ground for soul growth. The church is contrasted with the Sinai Baptist on the other end of the city, where the prosperous blacks can afford a more "muted benediction" to the Lord (62), a dry, soul-killing environment. Both of these churches reappear in *Linden Hills*. The names Canaan and

Sinai have relevant biblical meanings: Canaan's countryside was rich in fertile plains; Sinai, on the other hand, is part of the Saharo-Arabian desert and with annual rainfall that seldom exceeds 2.5 inches, the climate is arid. But no matter the church, Etta's dress is inappropriate for worship, displaying "too much bosom and too little dress" (62). The dress is a calculated move on Etta's part, however, for she is looking in earnest for a mate, one who will take her out of the race she has been running since she left Rock Vale thirty years earlier, a restless child of Ham (60). This biblical allusion refers to a story in which Noah is drunk and is seen naked by his son, Ham, the father of Canaan. When Noah discovers what had happened, he curses Ham and his future generations, declaring them the lowest of slaves (Genesis 9:25).

The invitation Etta sent out—dressed as "a bright red bird among the drab morality" (67)—was accepted by the one she most hoped would respond. The visiting preacher, the Reverend Moreland Woods, whose voice delivered a sermon that Naylor casts as far more than sexual foreplay, wants to play the game with Etta, who naively counts on the other not knowing that a game is already being played. Naylor's language emphasizes the delivery of the message over its content. The magnificent Reverend Woods sends out his threads which become a "pulsating organ" that with a certain amount of "push and pound" he turns into a "fierce rhythm," raises it to a "fevered pitch," and satisfies the congregation's unstated request: "fill me, fill me" (65). It may take long spasms in his chest, "sweat pouring down," and "trembl[ing] on the edge of collapse" on his part, but in the end, the congregation will find peace as they

sit back, "limp and spent" (66). Like the description of the conception of Brewster Place at the novel's beginning, Naylor's
language is intentionally sexually charged; Etta's invitation,
spoken without words, is a personal request for Woods to try
for the same effect in a different activity.

In the development of Moreland Woods, Naylor creates a
folkloric black preacher, whose three greatest character traits,
according to Nigel Thomas, are conning others, ostentation,
and lechery.[25] Woods' actions and manner display each of
these. Historically, the black preacher, because of his long
tenure of leadership, "dating back to the moment black people
were brought to this country as indentured servants and
slaves," has been the target of highest praise and lowest con-
demnation.[26] In Moreland Woods, Naylor makes little attempt
to develop him beyond a caricature. The deliberately sexual
language that describes his voice anticipates the sexual act
itself. Etta sees her salvation in a man like Woods as not spiritual, but earthly. When she expresses her hope to Mattie, who
has more clearly only seen the "opening gestures to a mating
dance" (70), Etta lashes out at her oldest friend.

Without Mattie's support, the game between Woods and
Etta begins. Naylor employs the language of a gambler—Etta
may win a few rounds, but "she would be bankrupt long before
the sun was up" and have only her body left to "place on the
table" (71). For Woods, who satisfied his congregation a half-
breath (66) before he reached his end, the delay in time creates
space for his full physical sexual release. Only when Etta
acknowledges this sexual drive consuming him, feels those
"last floundering thrusts," does she realize how solidly she has

lost the game. Just as with the preacher, she has been here before; the ending is no different, and she knows it even before she sees the locking doors that would be in his eyes (72).

All her life, Etta has been looking for a man, trying to "hook herself to any promising rising black star" (60). When one would dim, she sought another. Along the way, she lost the spunk that spirited her out of Rock Vale ahead of Johnny Brick's "furious pursuing relatives." She stopped defining herself alone and looked for definition within a coupling. Not asking more than that from life—to be one of two—she guaranteed herself frustration. She kept the Billie Holiday records in order to be reminded of the pain, to wallow in it. On her second return alone to Brewster Place within the day, her laugh, partially at least, acknowledges what she does have in reality—someone waiting for her. It is Mattie who has always been the constant and the comfort. Etta's dream has been deferred, but because of Mattie, it has not been killed.

## "Kiswana Browne"

From the summer day of Etta Mae Johnson's return, Naylor moves to an autumn hour during which Kiswana's mother comes to visit. This is a story about generational differences between mother and daughter set in the early 1970s with abundant references to the civil rights movement and the growing popularity of reclaiming African roots. On one level Kiswana is trying to adopt the spirit of the movement by choosing to live on Brewster Place and help her people, but on a deeper level Naylor exposes the naiveté of her awareness. Mrs. Browne represents everything that Kiswana, at this stage in her life, is dead set on rejecting. She is trying to make it on her own, but the freedom to do so comes with the cushion of a father with a "five-figure income and a home in Linden Hills" (83). Kiswana has embraced the cause of her people, much to the dismay of her mother who wants to distance these people from herself and from her daughter. Kiswana takes umbrage at the use of the word *these*, for she sees herself as one of them. They are poor, as is she, in her own mind. What her mother and the reader realize is that the other residents of Brewster Place do not have any other options.

Kiswana has dropped out of college, which in her defense she refers to as a bourgie school (83). However, she has had enough college education to understand Marxist theory at a rudimentary level and consequently has chosen to identify with the proletariat, the wage-earning class, as opposed to the bourgeoisie, the class which she now believes inhabits Linden Hills. Her college years were years spent fighting in the movement (84), a reference to the civil rights movement, which focused its energy on securing voting rights, access to public accommodations, and better educational and economic opportunities for blacks through nonviolent protest. The irony of the fact that she had the opportunity to be in college—one of the goals of the movement—and that she chose to drop out is lost on her.

By taking an African name, Kiswana has rejected her mother's choice in naming her Melanie. In doing so, she rejects her mother's attempt to honor her grandmother, "a full-blooded Iroquois . . . who bore nine children and educated them all, who held off six white men with a shotgun when they tried to drag one of her sons to jail for 'not knowing his place'" (86). When she drops the name Melanie, she loses a meaning that would fit her strong ethnic identity: black, of a dark complexion.[27]

Kiswana has acquired two pieces of art from Africa, an Ashanti print and a Yoruba goddess with large protruding breasts (82). At the time of the story's setting, African artifacts were just becoming available in the United States. Mrs. Browne's distaste for the suggestive wooden goddess (82) implies that she herself does not have extensive knowledge or awareness of African art, nor does she know Kiswana's lover, Abshu. When she tries to speak with Kiswana about male friends stopping by and warns of unpleasant situations that could be suggested by the Yoruba statue, she begins to stammer, as straight talk about sex makes her do. The stammering is repeated at the end of the story when Mrs. Browne takes off her new shoe to massage her sore foot and Kiswana notices and comments on the bright red nail polish (87).

In the hour of the visit, Mrs. Browne and Kiswana have talked at each other about the movement, African roots, and Kiswana's new name. In these discussions, Mrs. Browne is mature and articulate, while Kiswana is young and idealistic. Mrs. Browne clearly draws reader sympathy—not as a race representative but as a mother—when she expresses her disappointment at the name change. Kiswana understands her mother's comments but cannot articulate her response. The moment for Kiswana is overwhelming. Her mother's toenails become the medium through which the clearing in Kiswana's head can begin, for discovering the fact that her father had encouraged her mother to paint those nails, in Kiswana's mind, makes him into feet (87), exactly as is Abshu. Though she and her mother would or will never speak of what Naylor suggests they are both thinking, a healing has occurred for Kiswana. She sees herself with a new honesty—her activity with Abshu plows no new ground. As she looks at her mother, she sees "the woman she had been and was to become" (87).

## "Lucielia Louise Turner"

Ciel Turner is Miss Eva's granddaughter and Basil's early childhood playmate; Mattie is her second mother. Her presence on Brewster Place indicates a relationship gone sour, but the death of her only child is the real tragedy. In this fourth story, which is the first one Naylor wrote and published in *Essence* as "A Life on Beekman Place" two years before *The Women of Brewster Place* was completed and released, she employs another season and time. It is spring when Eugene returns to loiter about on the day of the funeral for his daughter, and it had been spring a year earlier when he had returned to Ciel after an absence.

In her story, Kiswana reminds the reader about Ben, the janitor, first introduced in "Dawn." She is relieved that he is not loitering about when her mother arrives, "sitting in his usual place on the old garbage can pushed against the far wall" (76). The first time Ben himself speaks, though, is in Lucielia's story, and his presence on that garbage can, as a kind of sagging sentry of Brewster Place, suggests the kind of man Eugene may one day become. Eugene and Ben are the only husband/father figures in the novel. Ben talks to himself, repeats a daily soliloquy (89); he is an actor, of sorts, who knows well that his role on the stage of life is to speak when or as if no one is listening, no one is present. When Eugene makes his first appearance on this spring day of his child's funeral, through Ben's besotted vision he is reduced to an "it" hesitating and an "it" hurrying over (89) towards Ben. The picture of Ben, whose story has not yet been told, creates an appropriate lost world for Eugene to enter.

Eugene's child will be buried on this day, but he does not feel welcome at the funeral. In this brief picture Naylor draws of him, she depicts a lost, broken, and emasculated man. He has become victim, and nothing about the death of his child is his responsibility. Mattie becomes his target—she is the ball-buster and the frig (90). Eugene sees Mattie usurp the role that he has abdicated, for he imagines her "rid[ing] in the limo, wearing the pants" (90). Naylor's choice of beginning with this anticlimactic moment pushes the reader, along with and through Ben, to remember Eugene's arrival a year before, when he did not hesitate but went in directly to see Ciel.

From Mattie Michael's story, the reader knows that when Miss Eva died, Ciel's parents came to take her away screaming (40). Part of the attraction—that unexplainable love (91)—Ciel feels for Eugene, even though he had deserted her and Serena for eleven months, has to do with his smell—"a deep musky scent . . . that brought back the ghosts of the Tennessee soil of her childhood" (92). Mattie, who has, as she told Etta, "banked them fires [of passion] a long time ago" (61), is hardly a candidate to whom Ciel can explain her feelings for Eugene. While Mattie clearly sees the explainable hate Ciel has for Eugene, she is out of the loop on the unexplainable love. Ciel's connection to Eugene through his smell, her ability to "inhale his presence," and to feel through her fingers his sooty flesh directly in her blood is intensely private (92). These feelings are not Mattie's business and, more importantly, while Ciel may know these things, it is likely she does not know them in language. In fact, the narrator's voice, speaking for Ciel, ponders, "how do you tell yourself" (92) and answers, "you don't" (92).

Like the oatmeal that manipulates time in Mattie's story, Naylor uses towels to pass time in Ciel's story. While folding towels, Ciel reviews the point at which tensions began to exist between her and Eugene. By the time the last towel has been folded, she knows that her announcement that she is pregnant is what altered Eugene's disposition. The towel reappears at the end of the story as both the thing itself when Mattie carefully dries off Ciel after her bath and as symbol of an arrival point at the end of Ciel's association with Eugene. As Naylor lets the explicit details of the sex between Mattie and Butch occur in his mind before the activity takes place, she also has Ciel predict exactly what Eugene is going to say and what she is supposed to say, and what it is supposed to lead to (93). Here, however, Ciel's anticipation of an expected chain of negative events precipitated by language causes her temporarily to avert their actuality.

The boiling water in the rice pot becomes Ciel's focus, as well as a symbol, when Eugene announces he has lost his job and spits out his ugly feelings about babies and bills (94). Each time Ciel changes the starch-speckled water and it becomes clearer, so does her understanding of Eugene's position. How-

ever, in the act of attempting to clear that water completely she
remembers that, ultimately, it will defeat her (94); the water
will never become completely clear. Eugene, too, will defeat
her with his position. He does not want this second baby; Ciel,
without speaking the words, understands that an abortion is her
only option. The unspoken gap that exists in the text is huge,
reflecting all that Eugene and Ciel do not say to each other.

In a careful placement, Naylor, using the same word, contrasts two sharply different moods. As she ends one paragraph,
Eugene is "shouting into [Ciel's] face" (95). The word *nothin'*
is repeated three times. The reader knows well that nothing is
what the baby will have to eat, but when Eugene speaks the
word *nothing*, he relates it not to the baby, but to himself. His
concern, rather than for Ciel, Serena, or the unborn baby, is for
his own status in the world. He is consumed with the driving
thought that he "ain't never gonna have nothin'" (95). This last
word—*nothin'*—in the paragraph is also the first word in the
next paragraph, which is separated by a space break in the text
to indicate passing time. This time the word emanates from a
genderless voice. *Nothing* is not being shouted at Ciel, and she
is not being grabbed and shaken; instead, "nothing to it" is how
much this "simple D&C" should concern Ciel (95). In discon-
necting the voice from its speaker, Naylor demonstrates the
cruelty of language and reminds the reader that Mattie would
gladly have chosen Basil's physically hitting her in the face to
the words he spewed at her (49).

That the voice should call Ciel "Mrs." Turner is significant, as Ciel's grandmother's name was Turner, and Ciel is her
son's child (34). It is unusual that Ciel would also marry a
Turner; therefore, if Ciel and Eugene are not married and the

title *Mrs.* is used by the voice deliberately, she is reminded of her insecure place, her lack of legal rights, in relationship to Eugene. Another person's automatic assumption that an abortion should be of no concern to Ciel denies her the opportunity to think differently. Because Ciel, in fact, does not want this operation, the only way she can endure the ordeal is to give it to some other woman (95). Unfortunately, that other woman lives inside Ciel, and the split consciousness with which Ciel moves through her days after the abortion prepares the reader for the complete crack and separation that Ciel experiences after the death of Serena, her only child.

When Ciel realizes that Eugene is going to leave her, in spite of all she had done in the name of love to play the game his way, the clearing in her head is instantaneous. It had been the other woman who wanted the abortion. The unexplainable love that she had felt for Eugene was wrapped up in his Tennessee smell that "lined the inside of her nostrils" (92), but the gangrenous poison moving through her body like a ferocious vacuum "drew his scent out of her nostrils and scraped the veil from her eyes" (100). Word choices—*drew . . . out, scraped*—suggest that Ciel aborts Eugene from her life. That sudden emptiness now must be immediately refilled with love; she has an "overpowering need to be near someone who loved her" (100). Ciel's realization appears to happen simultaneously with Serena's electrocution, for as she moves towards Serena to go to Mattie's, she hears the "scream from the kitchen" (101). Serena is old enough to play a game with a scampering roach, but too young to understand what sticking a fork into an electrical socket means.

Without Serena, Ciel gives up on life. After God refuses

her request to end her life, she takes the matter into her own hands. Refusing to eat, drink, or bathe, Ciel waits to die. When the community of women bring food and offer solace, their manifestations seem pitiful against Ciel's despair. Naylor creates a war zone with language to match this level of resignation, showing the power of words over physical acts of kindness. Throughout the novel, Naylor offers repeated examples of a character's preference for physical violence over certain groupings of words. Here language devastates—"impotent words flew against the steel edge of her pain, bled slowly, and returned to die in the senders' throats" (102). The first skirmish goes to Ciel, as does the second round: "[A neighbor woman] choked, because the words were jammed down into her throat by the naked force of Ciel's eyes, . . . raw fires [from Ciel's eyes] had eaten [the words] lifeless—worse than death" (102). It takes Mattie, who "loves [Ciel] too much" (95), to understand that words alone are not going to be her salvation. Mattie becomes the physical manifestation of the black Brahman cow (103), charging into the room to save Ciel's life. She says nothing, but she acts with no hesitation, refusing to let Ciel's will cut her down. Mattie responds to Ciel where she is, for the need Ciel has is "before-language." She grips her tightly enough to almost break her spine and begins to rock. Language has been pressed all the way down inside of Ciel, so far that she is impacted internally. To get that language out again, Mattie knows she has to first hear a moan. So she rocks. Naylor suggests that healing is connected to language, but to reconnect with language, forceful action may be necessary.

In the rocking, repeated a dozen times, Naylor presents a

metaphorical trip back through time, highlighting incidents where other mothers have sacrificed their children. Once Mattie gets past collective human history, she can rock Ciel back through her own personal history, back into the womb, in search of the nadir of the hurt (103); she creates a full body exorcism of the repressed evilness of pain (104) that exists inside Ciel. Throughout the whole of the rocking, the vomiting, and the bathing, Mattie does not say a word. The communication between the two women is solely in touch—one, the powerful giver and the other, the meek receiver. When the bath is finished, Ciel begins to cry her first tears since Serena's death.

The sobs that accompany those tears represent a movement toward language, a step removed from the moaning she did while being rocked. Mattie has managed through the force of her will, her love for Ciel, to unplug her, to direct her ongoing implosions outward. Ciel's tears are no longer steaming, killing her internal organs, but cold and good (105). Because the tears can come out now, Mattie knows that Ciel's exertion of energy will lead to sleep and, soon, morning would come (105). Morning is both the literal next day and the expectation that words and new hope will once again come from Ciel, a logical and possible progression from moaning and sobbing.

## "Cora Lee"

The four seasons and the increments of time that include a moment, day, hour, and year in the first four stories/chapters suggest that Cora Lee lives in a dream world outside of time and season. Even her location on Brewster Place is ambiguous;

Cora Lee and her seven children exist in the midst of chaos, supported by welfare and its food stamps. She resides somewhere between an irritable Miss Sophie, who lives on the first floor and shouts up the air shaft for the children to quiet down, and Kiswana Browne, on the sixth floor, who extends the invitation to Cora Lee and her brood to join her in the park at her boyfriend Abshu's production of *A Midsummer Night's Dream.* Naylor's choice of this particular Shakespearean comedy serves multiple purposes in Cora Lee's story, for Cora Lee, in spite of the reality of her growing children, lives in a dream world, acknowledging only what matters to her—the powerful attraction/addiction she has for babies.

Lines from three Shakespeare plays are quoted in Cora Lee's story, and all of them have to do with dreams. Naylor begins the story with lines from *Romeo and Juliet* (I.4.97–99), Mercutio's response to Romeo who reminds Mercutio that he "talk'st of nothing" (I.4.96) when he goes into detail of the previous evening's dream. Mercutio agrees with Romeo—that dreams "are the children of an idle brain / Begot of nothing but vain fantasy." Shakespeare's use of the word *begot* resonates perfectly with the shadows who begot through Cora Lee and suggests that her literal children are the end result of the activity of an idle brain. What follows is the exposition of Cora Lee's early attachment to new baby dolls and the talk from her mother that informs her she can make her own real babies with the "thing that felt good in the dark" (109). Her mother's warning not to repeat this activity had exactly the opposite effect because Cora Lee was desperate for babies.

In response to Cora Lee's information that what is necessary for having a baby is simply a crib and a little chest (120), Kiswana responds with the idle comment that babies grow up (120). This obvious statement registers with Cora Lee on some subconscious level as she reviews her six children's baby photo albums and realizes that the baby Sonya Marie must be photographed before it is too late (120). As Cora Lee flips randomly through the books that have frozen her children as babies, Shakespeare, having just been mentioned by Kiswana, returns to her mind. She associates "Maybelline's brown, infant eyes" (121) with a line from *The Tempest*—"We are such stuff / As dreams are made on, and our little life / Is rounded with a sleep" (IV.1.173–175). To Cora Lee, Maybelline was the stuff of dreams, but of late, she had become a "dumb ass," "left back," and "truant notices were coming" (111). Cora Lee's time and attention to the older child was constantly being redirected to her newest baby. The smell of the new child and the clarity of that baby's needs—"so soft and easy to care for" (111)—are what consumed Cora Lee, what she lived for.

The final Shakespeare play quoted is the one Kiswana has invited the whole family to attend with her. The quoted lines from *Midsummer Night's Dream* include yet another dream: "I have had a dream, past the wit of man to say what / dream it was" (IV.1.204–205). While Cora Lee watches the play, she casts a new reality for herself that everything would be different. The "truant nonsense" would stop, the children would attend summer school, she would check homework, and attend PTA meetings, and one day all her children, no longer babies, would have responsible jobs (126). The last quoted lines, however, make reference to *shadows,* a word that Naylor uses to refer to Cora Lee's lovers who come in the night to "show her the thing that felt good in the dark." As the playwright asks for pardon—"If we shadows have offended"—he also reduces the play to visions, calling it a "weak and idle theme, / No more yielding but a dream" (V.1.409–414). Shakespeare is used to help awaken, if only temporarily, Cora Lee from her dreams of babies. When Brucie sees the character Bottom wearing an ass's head (125), the sight makes literal what his mother is forever calling her children: "'Are you gonna be a dumb-ass too?' she cooed at the baby. 'No, not Mama's baby. You're not gonna be like them'" (113). Brucie worries that he will look like Bottom when he grows up. On this magical evening, she knows full well that babies do grow up. By the time she returns home, however, tucks all seven children in their beds, and joins "the shadow, who had let himself in with his key," she has "folded her evening like gold and lavender gauze deep within the creases of her dreams" (127). The colors and fabric used to describe the evening's being folded away are a description of the fairy people's costumes during the play (125). Like the play that was a vision, Cora Lee has returned to what she can salvage of the life she lives that is a dream—that she can make new babies.

Cora Lee comes to Brewster Place from a family that supported her as a child, giving her a new plastic baby doll each year. Her family is still present in her life. The sister who had lower marks in school (108) becomes the adult woman who lives in a big house in Linden Hills (121) and gives her the living room set that "only six months ago . . . was practically new" (116). Her mother is willing still to take a stand when she finds a reefer in Sammy's pocket, which someone from the park had given him (118). Early on Cora Lee's mother had warned her about "doing nasty" in the basement (109), but she does not vanish from her life when Cora Lee ignores her advice. The children's grandmother is a constant in their lives as all the flurry of activity in preparing to attend the play is first thought to be related to "grandma's coming over" (121).

While the family members remain present, they do not appear in the text in connection to Cora Lee's abuse from the father of her first two children. Cora Lee seems willing to accept the fractured jaw and loose tooth from this man with his gold-capped teeth and glass eye (113) for the household chores she could not get right, according to his demands. But when he smashes her face, which leaves her to carry the scar under her left eye because she could not keep a baby from crying, he had to go (113). Naylor's suggestion is that Cora Lee is willing to tolerate physical abuse for anything she did herself that was not pleasing to this man, but she is strong enough to put her foot down when the situation moves to the baby. Cora Lee's priorities are clear—the baby will come first, before herself, before any man. Cora Lee's hold on her babies echoes the way Ciel feels about Serena and even Mattie herself about Basil. The obvious difference is that Ciel, in her story, had aborted Serena's replacement, and Mattie, in her story, had only Basil, while Cora Lee cannot stop having babies. All three women, however, share an obsessive commitment to their children.

## "The Two"

The last of the seven women whose stories are told appears in the only story/chapter without a name in the title. Whereas Cora Lee existed in a dream state, Theresa and Lorraine exist in all seasons and through all lengths of time in the reality of being unwelcome in any place. While "the two" refers to the lesbian relationship of Theresa and Lorraine, the only women without last names, it is also a reference to the relationship of the janitor Ben and Lorraine. It is through this latter relationship that Lorraine becomes a more secure, self-defined person. During her stay on Brewster Place, Ben and Lorraine find solace in and with each other. The end of their story, however, holds death for both of them. The only mitigation for this profound sadness is that had both lived, they would have been different and stronger. The story also presents the community of women at its worst, as a precursor for the book's conclusion, which will present that same community at its best. Finally, the story contains C. C. Baker and his gang, the group that will gang rape Lorraine.

While Lorraine, the teacher, wants to be accepted by the neighbors—attend their neighborhood meetings, watch their children, exchange friendly conversation—her partner Theresa has no interest in the neighborhood where she lives. Lorraine, all softness, yearns for acceptance and lets others determine how she feels about herself. Theresa, on the other hand, is tough, works hard to see herself honestly and defines herself by knowing clearly who and what she is. While Theresa is self-defined, Lorraine is other-defined.

Theresa and Lorraine have come to Brewster Place not because they are economically deprived but because they are socially scorned, because Lorraine has felt the pressures of being denied normal status in former neighborhoods. Brewster Place is their last chance; there is nowhere else to go. In their stay here, it is Theresa who gradually becomes infected by what others think. During Theresa's food-throwing and screaming outburst (156–59), all that she says is directed to people who are *not* present. Theresa presumes to know what people are thinking, and in this scene, acts out her own internalization of Lorraine's fears. Her rage dissolves into sobs, and it is Lorraine who, in a reversal of roles, comforts Theresa.

The crux of the mounting tension that builds in their story has to do with being different. Lorraine is convinced they are not different, and Theresa insists they are. Theresa defines herself as a lesbian and uses the analogy of a cookie, which can be altered to be many other things, such as an earring, a Frisbee, a flying saucer, but it is still a cookie. As a cookie is a cookie, she is a lesbian. Naylor's choice of medium takes on a double meaning: in black slang, cookies are female genitalia.[28] And Theresa's appetite for chocolate chip cookies takes on a sexual meaning.

Lorraine chooses to see her life in a fullness beyond cookie status, and it is this conviction on her part that compels her to attend the neighborhood meeting. Miss Sophie, mentioned in passing in other stories, is developed in this final one. The first meeting of the Brewster Place Block Association takes place in Kiswana's apartment, where Mattie, Etta, and Cora Lee make an appearance, the first time in the novel that the community of women is together in one place. When Lorraine enters the room, the meeting disintegrates into Miss Sophie's homophobic diatribe against what she thinks of Lorraine's relationship. At this point Naylor reduces the lives of Theresa and Lorraine to only their sexual relationship, letting the "theys" of the world, as represented by Miss Sophie, have their say. At the meeting, Lorraine feels reduced to a cookie. It is Mattie, who first feels uncomfortable with the subject of women who love each other, but when she talks it out, she comes to the realization that "maybe it's not so different. . . . deep down it's not so different after all" (141). This awareness on Mattie's part prepares her for her role in comforting Lorraine as she dies.

At the meeting, however, Mattie is silent. Lorraine's simple offer to be the secretary turns into her own crucifixion. Sophie berates her, waves around the ebony statue, the weapon that she has plucked from Kiswana's apparently growing African art collection, and points it at Lorraine like a crucifix (145). And as at the crucifixion of Jesus when no one speaks against what is happening, this room is filled with silence, until Ben, the usually zooted janitor, steps forward. It is his language that abruptly stops Sophie's harangue. When Sophie tells of seeing Lorraine get out of the tub and call for Theresa to bring a clean towel, Ben retorts: "Guess *you* get out the tub with your clothes on, Sophie. Must make it mighty easy on Jess's eyes" (146).

Ben is the one who brings Lorraine down off that cross, where Sophie has tried to nail her, and takes her downstairs to his place. Ben, who has been silently present since "Dawn," reduced to only a drunkard by those people he lives among, moves to center stage through the developing relationship he builds with Lorraine. The reader finally hears him tell his own story. Ben's drinking is rooted in a pain through which he cannot move. Long ago he was a sharecropper in an unnamed southern state. His only daughter, crippled from birth, cleaned house for the white property owner. When his daughter tells him she is being sexually used by the white man, Ben is impotent in the situation; he can neither protect her nor prevent what is happening. Further, Ben has no support from his wife Elvira, who chooses not to believe their daughter, deciding instead to let Ben know what a failure he is as a man. Ben cannot defend himself to Elvira verbally, but he is perfectly articulate in his unspoken thoughts, which are all violent. He imagines "his big callused hands on the bones of her skull pressing in and in," or he wants to go in the house and get his shotgun and empty "the bullets into her sagging breasts" (153). When Ben's daughter leaves for Memphis and begins sending money home in envelopes with no return addresses, the unstated assumption is that she has most likely gone to Beale Street and become a prostitute. Ben drinks to fight the return of any part of the memory of his daughter's situation.

In Lorraine, however, his daughter is resurrected, for he notices that she walks not with a literal external limp but "sorta limped along inside" (148). And Ben became to Lorraine the resurrected father, for her own had "kicked [her] out of the house when [she] was seventeen years old" (148). Because Lorraine is able to "really, really talk" with Ben, she becomes a stronger, more confident person. In fact, she becomes what Theresa had earlier stated she hoped for—"someone who could stand toe to toe with her and be willing to slug it out at times" (136). When Theresa notices the changes in Lorraine, however, she is not sure she likes them. Even though she expresses some irritation with Lorraine when she sees Kiswana run interference for her during the street confrontation with C. C. Baker and his gang, Theresa herself had been ready to go to her aid. What Theresa says she wants (a strong woman) and what she really wants (Lorraine's continued dependence on her) send mixed messages to Lorraine. So when Lorraine resists going to the party that Theresa wants them both to attend, but ends up going by herself, she makes a definitive statement to her partner: "If I can't walk out of this house without you tonight, there'll be nothing left in me to love you" (167). Had Lorraine lived to see another day, her relationship with Theresa would have permanently changed. Theresa, who "would live to be a very old woman," cannot focus on what the two might have become. She is locked forever in attempting to recreate, recast the last words she might have said to Lorraine on that evening.

Naylor suggests that individually the boys that comprise C. C. Baker's gang can look in a mirror and see nothing, but collectively they mirror each other and can know they are alive. References to "their gods—Shaft and Superfly" are to two movies by these titles that were released in 1971 and 1972, respectively. *Shaft* is a formula private-eye plot in an all-black environment, and *Superfly* is an action-adventure film with drugs, sex, and violence, "the tale of a pusher with a heart of gold."[29] In the exchange that takes place between the boys and Kiswana and Lorraine in the street, Kiswana is able to "beat [C. C. Baker] at the dozens" (162), an elaborate word game of reciprocal insult. When Kiswana makes her comment which refers to the size of C. C. Baker's penis, she wins the game. In the mirror of his accompanying cronies he saw only respect for the girl (162). This confrontation, where Lorraine smiles at him, becomes the catalyst for the rape.

When Lorraine, back early from the party and not ready to face Theresa, makes her way through a back alley toward Ben's, she moves through C. C. Baker's territory. Naylor suggests that these boys know the extent to which they have power in the world, and it is limited to this alley in Brewster Place. The statement that "these young men wouldn't be called upon to thrust a bayonet into an Asian farmer"(169) hints, along with the dates of the movies, at the time of this scene. A few years earlier these boys would have been drafted and sent to Vietnam. It is at least 1972, and the military buildup in Vietnam is past. Sticking a pole into the moon (170), a reference to the first moon landing in July 1969 has also occurred. But what is left for them is an "erection to validate in a world that was only six feet wide" (170), the width of the alley they could rule.

Lorraine has never been with any man, and she does not want to hear about the men that Theresa had been with. Lorraine's strength had been increasing through her involvement with Ben, but now the physical desecration of her body through a gang rape that leaves only her eyes screaming for help destroys every bit of the person she was in the process of becoming, though not before she makes a final and desperate lunge at what she knows is movement (172). Nothing in the text states that Lorraine knows that movement is Ben; she sees only the motion on top of the garbage can (172). Ben is trying to get his own focus and precisely at the time he recognizes Lorraine, she slams the brick into his face. Usha Bande sees this moment as a symbolic killing of a father who rejected her and the repeated blows that follow as revenge for all those who have contributed to her misery.[30] However, Lorraine could just as easily believe that the movement she is aware of is by her rapists and her retaliation is exclusively directed to them for the violent crime perpetrated on her. She and Ben die together, and the proverbial chariot from the song that has haunted Ben, "Swing Low, Sweet Chariot," has finally arrived to carry the two of them home. At the end, "the two" are Lorraine and Mattie, as the raped one dies in the other's arms; Mattie remains the willing surrogate mother for each of Brewster Place's women in need.

## "The Block Party"

Lorraine's last words before dying are "Please, Please" (173), the plaintive cry at the end that sums up her life—please don't hurt me, please include me, please don't leave me out. It is a polite word, but in Lorraine's mouth, it becomes a begging, whimpering word, a word Theresa will live out her life avoiding. When Lorraine dies, her name is not spoken, as if to deny that she had ever lived. The rain that falls is charted from Ben's death. Sad as his death is, Ben's name can be spoken. For all the residents of Brewster Place, an eerie discomfort saturates their existence, hounds their erratic movements, and seeps into their sleep patterns. Even Mattie does not sleep well.

In Mattie's chapter/story, Naylor uses sleep as a means

through which time passes in reality. While oatmeal charts Basil's growth, time passes for Mattie by her continuous falling asleep on Saturday evening and waking on Sunday morning. At the end of the book, Naylor has Mattie fall asleep again so that time can pass in a wished for, out-of-reality way. Each of Brewster's residents has a dream that has been deferred, and these dreams are referred to throughout as disappointments, life's plans and hopes dashed. But in Mattie's literal dream, all the women of Brewster Place find resolution, solace, and, ulti- mately, vindication. Ciel returns, happy now, reports of a new man in her life, plans for a new baby. Within Mattie's dream, Ciel has dreamed of Ben and Lorraine, though she had left before "the two" moved in. Mattie has Ciel see Lorraine and herself as interchangeable, the blood on Lorraine's dress becomes red designs or red flowers (179). Mattie's subcon- scious is telling her that Ciel and Lorraine are not so different after all. Mattie, in her waking moments, had held each of them in her arms, had rocked them. One disappeared; one died. Ciel's presence in Mattie's dream allows Mattie to remember the good times—the innocent childhood of Ciel and Basil, Miss Eva and her cooking. Through Ciel, Mattie can speak of Basil, can make up what she needs to believe about his absence in her life: "[He] ain't run out of highway to stop and make him think" (178). Through Ciel, the one Mattie had helped reclaim her voice, Mattie can give language and, therefore, life to those people and times that sustain her in the present.

In Mattie's dream Etta gets her man. He is a handsome teenager, who dances Etta into the street where Mattie can see "hope . . . bouncing off swinging hips" (176). Etta becomes young once again, but even in Mattie's dream, she finds herself correcting Etta's false claims. Their friendship is, after all, one that "claimed co-knowledge of all the important events in their lives and almost all of the unimportant ones" (58). They will never see life the same way, and they will never completely stop trying to impose their views on each other.

In Mattie's dream Kiswana plays ball with Cora Lee's Brucie and turns to Mattie to express her concern about the rain. Kiswana and Mattie know little about each other. Kiswana has a mother of her own; her need for Mattie is insignificant in comparison with the others. To Mattie, Kiswana appears as the serious one whose goal is in earnest—make enough money at this block party to hire a lawyer to fight the injustices of an uncaring landlord. In Mattie's dream, Cora Lee is pregnant, and she reports to Kiswana that she is having weird dreams (181). Cora Lee bemoans the sad day her baby Sonya began to walk, speaks dismissively to Brucie; in short, Cora Lee is the same woman, doing what she does best—making another baby. This is the eighth baby; her story is redundant. Mattie, like Cora Lee's own mother, has offered advice in stopping Cora Lee's baby making—take how she started and practice reverse (123).

In Mattie's dream, Theresa is leaving Brewster Place, and nobody acknowledges her. Mattie, however, gives Theresa words to indicate that she is being affected by the "theys" of this world: "They're only having a lousy block party. And they didn't invite me" (187). After Theresa's loss, this thought is absurd, but it reflects Mattie's guilty conscience for her participation through silence in the lack of welcome extended to "the two."

In Mattie's dream, like the biblical claim—a little child shall lead them—Cora Lee's youngest, Sonya, is the one who discovers the stain on the brick, which she tries to scrape away with "a smudged Popsicle stick" (185). Under the control of Mattie's dream, Cora Lee delivers the brick to Mattie. By this time, however, all the men and children are huddled in the doorways, out of the rain and out of the way (185). The action centers on and with the women, while the men stand on the sidelines. The women take control of the moment, passing the stained bricks from woman's hand to woman's hand until the bricks are out of Brewster Place. Kiswana, the serious one, the one who is on Brewster Place by choice, resists involvement at first, but upon accepting the brick into her hands from Ciel, accepts these women as her equals; their fight is her own. Cora Lee delivers a brick to Theresa, who is trying to leave, and it is Cora Lee's use of the word *please* that snags Theresa: "Don't say that! . . . Don't ever say that!" (187). Theresa knew full well where *please* got her partner Lorraine, and in defiance of ever again having to yield to anyone else—man or woman— Theresa joins the other women with a vengeance. When she throws out her first brick, it bursts into a cloud of green smoke (188), the color of the dress Lorraine was wearing when she died. The body of the brick is shattered, but the spirit rises, like an ebony phoenix, so in this way Lorraine, too, appears within this common body. In Mattie's dream, all the women contribute to tearing down the wall, smashing through the barrier that cut them off from possibilities; no one is left out. The last line of Langston Hughes' poem, the book's epigraph, "Or does [the deferred dream] explode?" is demonstrated in violently graphic depiction. The answer is a resounding "Yes." But to explode is not to be destroyed. These women, as a community, will carry their dreams into another day. When Mattie wakes from this dream, the sun is shining.

# CHAPTER THREE

# *Linden Hills*

When *Linden Hills* was published during the first half of 1985, readers of Gloria Naylor's first novel were already familiar with the name of this wealthy residential subdivision, for it was located within sight of Brewster Place. Kiswana Browne, who lived on the sixth floor of 312 Brewster, could see her old neighborhood from her apartment window, a constant reminder of what she had chosen deliberately to give up in order to make it on her own with a group of women who had no other options. The reader also knows that Theresa of "The Two" once had an apartment in Linden Hills, and that Cora Lee's sister, the one not-so-bright as she, has a big house in Linden Hills. But nothing in *The Women of Brewster Place* prepares the reader for the Linden Hills Naylor presents in the novel that carries the name of the neighborhood.

As with the first novel, which Naylor begins with a description of the birth of Brewster Place, she chooses to launch *Linden Hills* the same way. The first Luther Nedeed, with his original 1820 survey had paid good money for land that was considered the "worthless northern face of a rich plateau."[1] The land-holding white farmers laughed at the "crazy nigger" who wanted to invest in "hard sod only good enough to support linden trees" (2). The joke that will backfire in the faces of the white establishment is similar to the beginning of Toni Morrison's *Sula,* for here, as well, white farmers believed they had played a "nigger joke" that resulted in their own "shucking, knee-slapping, wet-eyed laughter."[2] In Morrison's second novel, the "Bottom" becomes a neighborhood that used to be, and the emphasis is on the people who used to live there. With Naylor, the neighborhood that is conceived and comes to life through Luther Nedeed's design for the place remains as important throughout the novel as the characters who inhabit it.

One of the reasons for attaching such importance to the description of the place itself is Naylor's well-documented use of Dante's *Inferno.* In an early review in the *New York Times Book Review,* Mel Watkins makes the connection with Willie and Lester "(read Dante and Virgil), two young poets" and calls the novel "Miss Naylor's version of the 'Inferno,' . . . a much more ambitious work [than *The Women of Brewster Place*] in which realism is subordinated to allegory." But Watkins' review suggests that "because of the rigid allegorical structure, the narrative lists toward the didactic."[3] He sees Naylor's addition of material that does not appear to relate to the *Inferno* as weakening the effectiveness of the novel. On the other hand, writing for *Ms.,* Sherley Anne Williams says that Naylor "broadly transmogrifies Dante's *Inferno,*" but then engages the text in a wider context, suggesting that the bond between Willie and Lester "echoes, without imitating a similar one between the major characters [Guitar and Milkman] in Morrison's *Song of Solomon.*" Furthermore, she credits the way Naylor chooses to have Willa Nedeed discover the Mrs. Nedeeds who have come before her with the multiplicity of ways women's stories are salvaged and passed on, making a comparison with the letters Celie writes in Alice Walker's *Color Purple.*[4]

Joseph Brown, writing for *Callaloo,* calls the novel a cautionary tale and Naylor, "the descendant of Dante and Virgil and Eshu (the Yoruba god of the crossroads)." Asking if *Linden Hills* is the latest of books dealing with "the metaphor of a soul's journey into and through Hell," Brown wonders if the book, then, owes more to "Dante, or to Bunyan, or to Baraka" and answers, "all of the above . . . and then some." Brown argues that the *Inferno* is a hook, and the beast "waiting at the bottom of Linden Hills seeking whom he would devour is not the Lucifer of the Italian epic; he is the dragon of the Apocalypse [from] the Book of the Revelation of John the Apostle."[5] Joe Johnson, writing for *The Crisis,* associates Naylor's work with the "lyrical, impressionistic style of [Jean Toomer's] *Cane,*[6] while Sam Cornish, in the *Christian Science Monitor Book Review,* calls the novel "the darker side of the 'Bill Cosby Show.'"[7] Roz Kaveney in *TLS* sees the book in a vacuum, "thin in some of its textures" and Willie and Lester traverse, "in no especially symbolic sense, the Circles of Hell."[8]

In her second novel, Naylor chooses, as she does in the first one, to title her book with the specificity of place. The neighborhood conveniently takes its name from the linden trees that along with brier bushes grow down a steep, rocky incline (1). That the linden tree, historically, has been used for ornamental planting in order to beautify streets, that it has a light, soft, fine-grained white wood, and that, according to Greek legend, it is an emblem of conjugal love are all useful in understanding the neighborhood and its desirability. First, Linden Hills has grown from its early days, the brain child of the first

Luther Nedeed who conceived it. The fifth and present Luther reigns over the subdivision, granting deeds from his Tupelo Realty Corporation to those who have met the stringent qualification requirements. Like the linden tree, which now serves as part of the beauty of the physical landscape, the residents are a kind of ornament. They may not be white but they are making every effort to assimilate into American culture, leaving their blackness behind if it prohibits them from a prestigious address in Linden Hills. Being married to the "right" kind of person assists the candidate toward that address.

In the Greek legend, Philemon and Baucis, the classical Phrygian couple of wedded love, were allowed by Zeus to die at the same moment, and their bodies were changed to trees—Philemon became an oak, and Baucis, a linden tree. According to the folklore of the linden tree, the qualities of a tender wife unite in this tree—beauty, grace and simplicity, softness of manners, and an innocent gaiety. In the spring, the tree is covered with a delicate greenness, emits an enticing fragrance, and yields its blossoms to the visits of bees. The shade of the linden tree is the place of gossip and romance.[9] What constitutes an acceptable wife in modern Linden Hills is more akin to the wife of legend than a capable, independent woman.

Linden Hills becomes a metaphor for a Faustian pact with the Devil Nedeed. Lester and Willie are the reader's guides as they illustrate through their own discovery one person after another's willingness to sacrifice personal dreams—in love, in careers, and in leisure activity—for a downward movement through the circular drives. Each is striving toward the ultimate of addresses in this inverted and perverse world. These characters seem oblivious that their destination—where the proprietor's name spelled backwards, de eden—is only an ironic reminder of whence and how far they have fallen. Because the people of Linden Hills, individually, represent a myriad of ways in which the fall can take place, looking at their individual stories explains *Linden Hills.* These people, as a neighborhood, do not need each other; their lives do not depend on nor are they involved with each other. Where a character's issues or concerns naturally conjoin with another, they will be discussed as a group here. Such is the case beginning with all the Luther Nedeeds, moving to Willie and Lester, Ruth and Norman, all the Tilson women, David—Winston—Cassandra, Xavier and Maxwell, Lycentia and Chester Parker, Rev. Michael T. Hollis, Laurel Dumont, Daniel Braithwaite, and concluding with all the Mrs. Luther Nedeeds.

The physical description of Linden Hills is deliberately similar to Dante's *Inferno.* Here is a map of where people live in Linden Hills. In an allegorical reading, their addresses suggest their sins. First Crescent Drive is Dante's first circle of the unbaptized (Lester Tilson); Second Crescent is the second circle of the lustful (Winston Alcott); Third Crescent is the third circle of the gluttonous (Xavier Donnell); Fourth Crescent is the fourth circle of the misers and the wastrels (Chester Parker); Fifth Crescent is the fifth circle of the delivering angel (Rev. Michael Hollis). Tupelo Drive is a combination of the last three of Dante's circles—a place for suicides (Laurel Dumont), hypocrites (Daniel Braithwaite), and traitors (Luther Nedeed).

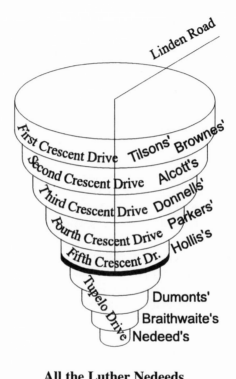

## All the Luther Nedeeds

Naylor creates five Luther Nedeeds, each one having a solitary son, but she does not detail each of their stories. Collectively, they appear as a continuum; each one, virtually indistinguishable from the one before, responds to history as it unfolds around him. The Luther of 1820 buys the land and defies, through the power of his eyes and his demeanor, intrusion from anyone as he gives birth to his dream. In Genesis, God speaks the world into existence in seven days and comments on its goodness. Sitting in the dead center of the lowest point of Linden Hills, Luther, in the same amount of time, thinks his world into a plan and projects its birth by closing his eyes at the end of his vigil and smiling. Because this Luther reads well the world in which he lives, he knows how to play its game, understands the role of blacks in a world dominated by whites. He is, after all, in the North and knows that blacks and whites may not live together, but may be buried together. In the South, from where he came, blacks and whites could neither live nor be buried together. With this knowledge and the proximity of his land to the town cemetery, he becomes an undertaker. Along with burying the dead and knowing that all people must live and die, he builds shacks along the upper part of the wedge of land and rents them out. By 1837 he returns to Tupelo, Mississippi, to find an octoroon wife, who bears him a son. For the next 42 years until his death in 1879, Luther pursues his business along with his son once he comes of age. Together they are referred to as big frog and little frog (4).

As a young man, the second Luther supplies guns to the Confederacy, an action that supplants a moral conscience with a greed for material gain. This Luther rents shacks on Tupelo Drive, builds a moat around the expanded Nedeed home, and begins the sale, "practically for air" (7), of land to the people who were renting, with conditions attached. These people may sell to another black, pass the property to their children, or forfeit the place to the continuing line of Luthers. At this point in the history of Linden Hills, the decision to offer the thousand-year-and-a-day lease was to keep the land in the hands of black people, and any black person would do. The government and real estate developers, other than Luther himself, of course, were clearly seen as the white enemy.

The third Luther, the most vaguely drawn, plays the role of a conjunction, connecting his grandfather and father to his son, the fourth Luther, who deals with the Great Depression. This Luther knows the world is heading white and, for him, Linden Hills takes on a new dimension—"a beautiful, black wad of spit right in the white eye of America" (9). It becomes the job of the fourth Luther to correct the second Luther's giving away the land. The houses must be owned by the "right" kind of people—just any black person will no longer fit the design. The people that cannot live in Linden Hills would be "madmen like Nat Turner or Marcus Garvey" (11). These historical figures helped reshape popular opinion. In 1831, Turner led the only effective slave revolt in America. With his fierce hatred of slavery, he dispelled any notion of the contented slave. Garvey, referred to as the Black Moses, was the charismatic leader of the Universal Negro Improvement Association (1916–1927), which harbored, but later aborted, plans to build in Africa a black-governed nation.

The fourth Luther understood that material goods mattered, that their accumulation spelled success, and that turning Linden Hills into an ebony jewel (9) would be his method of making the white world squirm. In the white folk, this Luther wanted to "spawn dreams of dark kings with dark counselors leading dark armies against the white god and toward a retribution" (10). Naylor's association of kings with counselors echoes Job 3:14, where Job curses the day he was born and wishes he could be at rest "with kings and counselors of the earth who rebuild ruins for themselves." Job utters the line out of a deep sense of resignation; Naylor's reference imposes that resignation on a forlorn white world that should tremble at the "brilliance . . . of what the Nedeeds were capable" (10).

The fourth Luther lived long enough to see Linden Hills become a district of eight circular drives, the same number of circles that Dante uses in his *Inferno*. In direct correlation, Naylor plays out the geographical grid of her neighborhood to parallel Dante's Hell. First, the top five streets are called First through Fifth Crescent Drive. The first five drives are divided from the lower three by street name—Crescent to Tupelo—and geographical protuberance—"the entire bottom of the land is hemmed in by the town cemetery" (2). In Dante's Hell, the first five circles are hemmed in by the River Styx and the Walls of Dis. The lower three are more complicated as the seventh circle contains three rings and the eighth circle has multiple levels, all decreasing in length as they lead to a ninth circle at the center, which is the home of traitors, the heart of Dante's Hell. Tupelo Drive, for which the fourth Luther ventured to Washington to maintain its name, leads continually downward to its center, the home of all the Luther Nedeeds, traitors every one. The President this Luther has on his side, "the socialist with his nigger-loving wife" (14) is a reference to Franklin and Eleanor Roosevelt.

When *Linden Hills* begins, all of these Luthers are dead. The one who reigns supreme during the development of the

novel is the fifth Luther. As the last of the Luthers on the continuum, this one adds his knowledge to the reader's information base. He sees the difference in the dream of the Luthers
before him—to have Linden Hills reflect some greatness back
on the Luthers—and his awareness of the reality that there is no
white god at whom to shake a fist: "Linden Hills wasn't black;
it was successful" (17). The people who continue to send in
applications to Linden Hills, to gain entry into a place that
would show the world they had made it, to move downward to
prestige only to vanish, got lost in the process of their own
arrival. The white world they had once held in contempt was
now an ally. Along the way, the act of acquiring the address
and the material comforts that accompanied it replaced everything that really mattered. The fifth Luther knew this because
he alone "wondered why none of the applicants ever questioned the fact that there was always space in Linden Hills"
(18). These are hollow people.

The fifth Luther is the father of the sixth Luther, the child
that he does not believe is his own, so he creates the conditions
that bring about the child's death. He also creates the conditions that eventually will, at story's end, cause his own death,
terminating the 150–year continuum of a Nedeed design.
Nedeed's function in the novel is the exact opposite of Mattie
Michael's role in *The Women of Brewster Place*. She is everywhere present, the surrogate mother, or ready to be, to all the
women. She is the force behind the community, the never-
ending source of good will. Similarly, Nedeed is everywhere
present, but his participation in the community is perverse and
evil. He is a father who kills with a plan that can only lead to

destruction for all. Mattie, in her spirit, is the largest of the ebony phoenixes; Nedeed, in his spirit, is doomed and what he assumes will never come, "the cold day in hell," will take him in the end.

## Willie and Lester

Naylor's choice of names—Willie K. Mason and Lester-field Walcott Montgomery Tilson—for the two who serve as the reader's guides through Linden Hills suggest a comic allusion to the black ventriloquist Willie Tyler and his dummy with an exaggerated Afro, Lester. Tyler, a soft-spoken person, has called Lester his alter-ego, using the dummy to say things that Willie cannot say for himself. Naylor's Willie uses Lester in much the same way. When his mouth gets him in trouble during the visit to Norman and Ruth's, Willie looks to Lester for help (38).

Willie and Lester also serve as the Dante and Virgil figures, respectively, of the novel. When Dante (1265–1321) was a young man, Italy was almost always under siege. His family was connected in Florence to the Guelphs, a papal party antagonistic to the Ghibellines. The Guelphs split into two factions, the Blacks and the Whites. As a White, Dante was forced into exile by his political enemies in the other faction. For the last twenty years of his life, he lived outside of Florence, wrote *The Divine Comedy,* traveled, and lectured. Willie's nickname, White, given to him because he was "so black that the kids said if he turned just a shade darker, there was nothing he could do but start going the other way" (24), is an ironic physical reminder of what Willie is not, and a link to Dante's political faction.

Just as Virgil serves as the guide to Dante in the excursion through Hell, Lester serves as the one who makes it possible for Willie to have easier access to Linden Hills because Lester and his family live on First Crescent Drive. The first circle of Hell, Limbo, where the unbaptized dwell because they preceded Jesus Christ, is Virgil's home in the afterworld. As Dante knows Virgil's poetry, Willie first reads Lester's poems before he admits to his friend that he also is a poet. Naylor's use of poetry becomes a vehicle larger than only a connection to the *Inferno,* for Willie and Lester are contemporaries and their knowledge that the other finds solace in writing poetry deepens their friendship: "Giving sound to the bruised places in their hearts made them brothers" (28). Willie keeps his poetry in his head because "his aim was to be like the great slave poet, Jupiter Hammon, who memorized thousands of verses because he couldn't read" (29). Hammon (1711–1806?) published nine pieces of prose and verse, and on each of them he indicated that he was "a Negro Man belonging to Mr. Joseph Lloyd."[10] Though Willie's claim for Hammon is that he could not read, critics have indicated that Hammon was "allowed to acquire skills of reading and writing in the early eighteenth century so that he could assist his masters in commercial endeavors."[11] Willie's formal education stops in the ninth grade.

Willie and Lester have been friends since they were in the seventh grade at Wayne Junior High School. When they meet in front of that school the week before Christmas, they are 20 years old. The words on the bronze plaques over the school's triple doors are a parody of the opening three lines of Canto III of the *Inferno*. When Naylor's lines are placed beside a translation of Dante's, the ironic inversion is clear:

| | |
|---|---|
| I am the way out of the city of woe — | Through me you enter the woeful city, |
| I am the way to a prosperous people — | Through me you enter eternal grief, |
| I am the way from eternal sorrow — | Through me you enter among the lost. |
| Sacred justice moved my architect — | Justice moved my high maker: |
| I was raised here by divine omnipotence — | The divine power made me, |
| Primordial love and ultimate intellect — | The supreme wisdom, and the primal love. |
| Only the elements time cannot wear — | Before me nothing was created |
| Were made before me, and beyond time I stand — | If not eternal, and eternal I endure |
| Abandon ignorance, ye who enter here (44) — | Abandon every hope, you who enter.[12] |

Willie's comment as he looks at the last plaque indicates that he takes the last line seriously. He knows that he should have stayed in school. He has memorized 665 poems, a number that is only one away from the number of the beast, 666, in Revelations 13:18. Hebrew and Greek letters have numerical equivalents, and the sum of the separate letters of the Antichrist's name equals the number 666.

The poets Willie has memorized—Amiri Baraka (1934– ), formerly Leroi Jones, a man who represents the revolutionary mood of the 1960s and changed his name after Malcolm X was assassinated; Wole Soyinka (1934– ), a Nigerian poet and playwright, well versed in the Yoruba culture, who received the Nobel Prize for Literature in 1986; and Langston Hughes (1902–67), who was in the vanguard of the Harlem Renaissance—were prolific poets. Their complete canons along with most of Samuel Taylor Coleridge and Walt Whitman (45) total more than 665, a number Naylor mentions at least three times (44, 45, 275), a reminder of its proximity to the beast's number. When Willie composes his poem about the "man in a house at the bottom of a hill" (277), he has 666 poems in his head. The last one is about the Antichrist figure in this novel.

In many ways, Willie is the central character. Through him, the reader discovers the unfolding world of Linden Hills' secrets. Naylor's placement of every detail—the addresses of the houses where Lester and Willie do chores double as allusions to the *Inferno,* the simple act of their spending the night together, and the placement of Willie's dreams—predicts what is to come. As they move through the neighborhood, like Dante and Virgil moving downward in hell, Naylor is careful to identify by address each person for whom the boys work. When Lester invites Willie to his home for the night so that they can get an early start in the morning, the two spend the night in the same bed. Naylor suggests the physical contact they have with each other is the result of innocent sleep patterns; Henry Louis Gates, Jr., on the other hand, explores their connection as homoerotic. Citing examples from the trepidation of divulging their poetry to each other to spending this night in bed together, a night that deliberately precedes the wedding of the declared gay Winston, Gates makes a case for Willie as the sexual cynosure in the novel.[13]

Linden Hills is Lester's neighborhood, and like Virgil who knows Hell and makes the offer to Dante, he is willing to be Willie's host and his guide. Naylor draws Lester as more worldly-wise than Willie. Lester has inherited his grandmother's cynical attitude about Linden Hills. He believes he can see through the hypocrisy of his mother, his sister Roxanne, and her boyfriend. Lester shares Kiswana Browne's view of the world. This young woman, who abandoned the best house on First Crescent Drive for a studio apartment on Brewster Place, was declared by Lester's mother to be "mentally disturbed . . . putting holes in her nose, taking some heathen name" (28). But when Kiswana comes collecting clothes for the Liberation Front in Zimbabwe, Roxanne's comment to her "that the people of Zimbabwe weren't ready for independence" sends Kiswana away quickly and embarrasses Lester. To the chagrin of both sets of parents, Kiswana has chosen to drop out of college, and Lester has chosen not to start. The offspring of First Crescent Drive dwellers understand what the fifth Luther Nedeed banks on nobody knowing—that "they've lost all touch with what it is to be *them*. Because there's not a damned thing inside anymore to let them know" (59).

Lester's cynicism is deepened by his preoccupation with Malcolm X. Though Willie suggests that Malcolm X could be offended by Lester's using his mother's hospitality and insulting her to her face, Lester chooses to express his frustrations of life in Linden Hills by listening to tapes of Malcolm X, an alternate voice to Martin Luther King's during the civil rights movement. With Malcolm's poster on his bedroom wall and a three-foot stack of his taped speeches at the foot of the television stand, Lester chooses "Message to the Grass Roots" to play for Willie. Malcolm X delivered this speech to the Detroit Council for Human Rights several weeks before the November 1963 assassination of President John Kennedy. The fact that Lester listens to—instead of reads—these speeches encourages an antagonistic attitude within him. According to one critic, listening to Malcolm X is "vastly superior to the written text in conveying style and personality of Malcolm at his best—when he was speaking to a militant black audience."[14]

The first dream that Willie reports having, the one that drives "him toward the security of his friend's body" (72), occurs the night before the boys' descent into Linden Hills. Naylor's choice of language predicts the next day's story: Winston, who loves David, chooses to abandon that partnership for the respectability of marriage to a woman he does not love. Willie's "night images . . . the flashes of a huge clock with snakes and spiders for hands and numbers" (72) are similar to Dante and Virgil's meeting with Minos. As a clock would strike time to Willie and Lester, telling them that work awaits this day on Second Crescent Drive, Minos stands inside the second circle, where Hell proper begins, horrible and snarling, listening to sinners confess and determining, by girding himself with his tail, where exactly in Hell the sinner will be sent.[15]

Willie's second dream occurs after overeating Parker's leftover roast beef and Nedeed's cake. Pale hands with bright red fingernails "growing and curling like snakes around the cake" reach out to him from a long row of erect coffins as he runs through a glass door and down a dark corridor (145). It is the morning he will go to Fifth Crescent Drive. Similarities exist in Canto IX of the *Inferno,* in the corresponding fifth circle. Dante is confronted by three hellish Furies, who beat their breasts and tear at themselves with their nails. They have snakes for hair, and Virgil covers Dante's eyes for him to pass by safely. Willie alone in his dream has no option but to run straight ahead, "trying to avert his eyes from the ghostly fingers [and] bloody snakes" (145), move through the glass door, and wake up in his bed. As in I Corinthians 13:12, Willie sees through the glass darkly, but all too soon, he will see face to face; he will come to know more about the world reflected in Linden Hills. His seeing clearly, however, will have to wait, for in his third dream Willie is told by the saleswoman from whom he tries to buy a Disc camera that he has no face (211). It is a dream that prevents him from trying to return to sleep in the early hours of the day he and Lester begin their descent onto Tupelo Drive, a day in which he will encounter Laurel Dumont, whose face disappears in her fatal dive into an empty swimming pool.

## Ruth and Norman

Ruth and Norman Anderson are an exemplary model of a happily married couple; it is significant that they make their home outside of Linden Hills. The names Naylor has chosen correspond with the names of a real-life exemplary couple, Ruth and Norman Vincent Peale (1898–1993). Peale, longtime minister of the Marble Collegiate Church in New York

City, wrote one of the most popular books in publishing history, *The Power of Positive Thinking* (1952). Through positive thinking, Ruth and Norman manage to put the best possible spin on their relationship and live together in full awareness that "love rules in this house" (38).

Because this fictional Norman suffers every other spring from the pinks, a disease that makes him feel as though he must gouge himself with every available hard object that he can reduce to a scraping surface in order to remove the pinks from his skin, the couple keep only a minimum of furnishings in their apartment. Ruth stays with this man because of some aspirin and a glass of water (37) which he manages to bring to her while he is being attacked by the pinks. His determination to help her when she is sick overrides his own desperate need to claw the pinks away from his skin. Naylor's choice of this color for Norman's disease has echoes throughout Linden Hills and is a way of warning the couple and the reader what is best avoided in that neighborhood. In the loveless wedding of Winston and Cassandra, they ride to the church in a car decorated with pink and white crepe paper (80); Xavier attends that wedding with a woman in a pink satin suit (83); Willie thinks the new furniture for Chester's bride-to-be will be psychedelic pink (129); Lycentia is buried in a pink dress (184); the blood stains that Laurel leaves on the snow are pink and beige (249); and Willa's first memory of herself is in a pink ruffled dress (277).

Naylor's choice of the name *Ruth* also matches with the biblical Ruth, whose declaration to her mother-in-law Naomi after her husband's death reflects this same selfless message about love that is the mainstay of Norman and Ruth's relationship: "But Ruth said, 'Entreat me not to leave you or to return from following you; for where you go I will go, and where you lodge I will lodge; your people shall be my people, and your God my God'" (Ruth 1:16).

Ruth is also the ideal fantasy love interest of Willie, the Beatrice figure to Dante. Ruth is the person willing to arrange the work opportunities for Willie and Lester, while Willie's ability to talk coherently, to behave normally melts in her presence. Many critics believe that Dante's beloved woman was Beatrice Polinari, a woman whom he had known most of his life but with whom he had little contact. She married Simone de'Bardi and died when she was twenty four. When Matthew Arnold explores Dante's connection with Beatrice, he suggests that she became such an inspiration precisely because she was not accessible: "To have had his relations with Beatrice more positive, intimate, and prolonged, to have had an affection for her into which there entered more of the life of this world, would have even somewhat impeded, one may say, Dante's free use of these relations for the purpose of art."[16] Willie responds to Ruth with supreme reverence. When he dreams of her, Ruth lies naked on his bed, while he stands over her with "no desire or need within him to touch her, just a heady contentment in watching her" (31).

Ruth's line—about love ruling their home—to Willie and Lester when they are visiting her and Norman's apartment on that cold winter night before they begin their work echoes the language and sentiment of Beatrice during her first appearance in the *Inferno:* "I am Beatrice who send you. . . . Love moved me and makes me speak."[17] Beatrice is compelled to speak by love, which rules in her head and heart, and she implores Virgil to help Dante because she fears that he, left alone, may turn away in fright. Without Lester, Willie could not begin the week of odd jobs in Linden Hills. When Willie and Lester make their way from the Crescent Drive area into the Tupelo area, they are stopped by police officers who question their right to be where they are. During their discussion with the police, Norman arrives and rescues them, doing so because "Ruth had a feeling that [they] might get [themselves] into a mess, walking around down here" (198).

Through Willie's eyes, Ruth has unearthly powers. She transforms styrofoam cups into china, and cheap blackberry brandy into a rare cognac (33). Willie finds himself tongue-tied in her presence, and when he accidentally suggests pink as the next color to paint the apartment, Ruth's look withers him. He loses the capability to smile, and he wishes he could "crawl across the floor to Ruth on his knees, bury his head in her lap, and beg her to forgive him" (39). He frets that never again will he hear "the smallest of music from that throat" (39). When he hears Ruth rage about Linden Hills, using a curse word, Willie speculates that she will use the same language about him: "Came in my house and had the gall to insult my husband—the black bastard" (40). Willie resorts to self-flagellation because he has let the word *pink* slip innocently, but thoughtlessly, from his mouth; he wishes he could die. His response to Ruth is excessive. Lester knows this and tries to lighten Willie's mood with crass language about Ruth to which Willie can only retaliate as a gentleman and courtly lover: "That's a *lady,* dammit! And she's too good for you to be wiping your greasy mind all over her body. You ain't worth six inches of her toenails. She's a saint" (43). Dante's similar, yet differently expressed, obsession with Beatrice appears in his early work, *La Vita Nuova,* where he explores his love-in-grief.

Ruth and Lester share a haunting suspicion about Linden Hills. Ruth, for a period of six months in an earlier marriage, lived on Fifth Crescent Drive. The counterpart in the *Inferno* is inhabited by the wrathful. Those who once "account[ed] themselves great kings" are now "furious shades" who "lie like swine in mire, leaving behind them horrible dispraises."[18] The novel provides no information about Ruth's former husband, but their address, read alongside Dante's masterpiece, suggests everything the reader needs to know about why Norman is preferable to this earlier mate. When Norman speaks of applying for a house in Linden Hills, Ruth wants no part of it, claiming the "folks just aren't real" (39). Lester agrees wholeheartedly, acknowledging that the people who do live there "are a bunch of the saddest niggers you'll ever wanna meet" (39). Both Ruth and Lester speak from inside knowledge, and they say it aloud to each other and to the outsiders Norman and Willie when they are conveniently not inside Linden Hills.

Demeaning talk of the upscale neighborhood from the Andersons' dilapidated garden-apartment building (33) is safe. But as warm and cozy as the apartment is, Ruth is the one who hears through the closed windows and the walls the thin howl that makes the hair stand up on their arms (42). Norman believes it is a sick animal, but Ruth knows better, and it is Lester who places the eerie sound exactly in the right location: "Maybe old Nedeed's down there embalming someone who wasn't quite ready" (42). Lester becomes the provider of foreshadowing information; he is the character to whom the reader must really listen. While his comments seem dismissive, they are loaded with literal accuracy and information that is useful at a later time.

Before Willie and Lester leave the Andersons' place this night, Willie has received absolution from Ruth. She has not only suggested that the boys could make money from doing spare jobs for people in Linden Hills, but she blesses Willie in her proposed endeavor by placing her hand on his shoulder (41). The benediction she utters is one that attempts to put modern materialism—the driving pursuit of Linden Hills' characters—in its rightful place: "I hate to see you looking so sad just because of money" (41). On the literal level, Willie's parting thought is highly dramatized, but his words are appropriately ironic in Naylor's use of the *Inferno:* "He was just sorry that she hadn't asked him to go into hell for her so he could really prove himself" (41). Finally, after being sent forth from Ruth, the chastened and forgiven Willie appears ready to take the communion wafer: "Willie swallowed to dissolve the joy in his throat from her touch" (41). When the boys take their leave from Norman and Ruth, her departing words are a warning of "Dobermans and wired fences. . . . and things like that" (42). While Beatrice encourages Virgil to be Dante's guide, Ruth gives the warning to Lester; she knows that without Lester, Willie has no license in Linden Hills.

## All the Tilson Women

The two women who dominate Lester's life are his mother and his sister, Roxanne; however, the greatest influence comes from the memory of his now deceased paternal grandmother, Mamie. She is the woman to whom the thousand-year lease was granted by the third Luther, the same woman from whom the fourth Luther tried to take it back. Lester's grandmother knew three generations of Luthers and their evil ways (12). Through her, Lester has developed his healthy skepticism of the neighborhood and its proprietor. Each of these women represents a different response to making it in Linden Hills and serves as a vehicle by which Naylor moves through chronological time and through the desire for descending in the neighborhood: Grandmother detests everything about it; Mother wants something more for her children; and Sister, who fully understands the rules, cannot move fast enough towards this end. Mother and sister bear a faint resemblance to the second and third beasts Dante encounters while lost in a dark wood: the lion and the she-wolf. The lion, representing pride, "appeared to [Dante] and seemed to be coming at [him], head high and raging with hunger"; the she-wolf, representing power and wealth, "seemed laden with every craving."[19] Willie hesitates before going to Lester's home, knowing that Mrs. Tilson has never been too keen on him (46), and that Roxanne's determination to "marry black, marry well—or not at all" (53) is the essence of materialism that both Willie and Lester despise.

Lester's antipathy toward Linden Hills has been supported by his grandmother. Through her, Lester has been willed the house because "she knew [he'd] do the right thing after [his] mom dies, and burn it to the ground" (46). Mamie Tilson is the fourth Luther's nemesis; he calls her the "one flaw deep in the middle of his jewel" (13). The first information the reader is given about her is that she fished with the third Luther, the Luther in the chain of them about which the least is spoken. But Mamie is no one's fool; she apparently fished for the money, for this third Luther paid her "five dollars to catfish with him cause the fish would run from his hook, . . . but he'd pay double that just for her catfish heads" (40). Mamie is in apparent complicity with Luther's obsession with catfish heads because she knows enough to be repulsed by his evil ways (12). However, the reader must wait until the fifth Luther hacked off the head of a catfish and carried it "out the back door to his mortuary and the body of Lycentia S. Parker" (70) to understand that the obsession with catfish heads is related to his necrophilic attraction. The narrative line suggests that at least the third, fourth, and fifth Luthers all use these heads to satisfy their perverse attraction to the dead.

Mrs. Tilson married into Linden Hills, albeit to the smallest house on the least prestigious street, and has spent a lifetime wanting "a better life for [her] children than [she] had" (50). She represents the naively blind—one whose intentions are well meaning and sincere, but who cannot realize how her efforts affect those around her. When she pours out her story to Willie, he sympathizes with her, but Lester speaks for his father, who at his mother's goading never had more than four hours of sleep a day for ten years in spite of his heart condition. She always wanted more; Lester thinks of her as the one who "killed [his] father. . . . and want[s] to choke her" (52). Lester has only this one way of seeing his mother, but he lives under her roof, eats her food, sleeps warm, and keeps clean through her services on his behalf. When he and his sister argue at the table, it is his mother who reminds them of their manners. They owe an apology to Willie because he is a guest, and "only the crudest people are rude to their dinner guests" (56). Willie's response to her moves back and forth between positive and negative. As soon as he feels "a flood of regret for every bad thought he'd ever had about Mrs. Tilson," he takes a final glance over his shoulder only to see her "mouthing something behind her hand to Roxanne" (56).

The Tilson home on First Crescent corresponds to Dante's first circle of Hell or Limbo, where the unbaptized dwell, the home of Virgil. Mrs. Tilson has decorated her home in green—willow-green print furniture, jade carpeting, green and white Japanese porcelain vases, avocado stripes and fern prints on the curtains, emerald satin balls on the Christmas tree. As Virgil shows Dante the lay of the land, the great spirits are gathered "on the enameled green." When the two descend into Hell, they lose this color, for Hell is not a "meadow of fresh verdure."[20] Once Willie and Lester venture onto Second Crescent, they, too, leave behind the green world.

Roxanne Tilson is the representative for everything desired by the younger generation of African-American women. On paper, she has all the credentials for the slide onto Tupelo Drive: a B.A. degree from Wellesley, a Linden Hills address—because "you don't get a Park Avenue husband with a Harlem zip code" (53), tasteful clothes, "a decade's worth of bleaching creams and hair relaxers" (53), a professional position; however, she lacks the one thing she needs to make it. Roxanne needs a man to marry, for in Linden Hills, marriage is necessary for moving down. In her search for success as Linden Hills and her mother have helped her to define it, Roxanne loses the ability to cherish her own values. Though the assumption is that the position she holds in the world of work was made possible through an education at Wellesley, the black history courses in which she enrolled while there are reduced to supplying "her with the statistical proof that black men were further behind white men than ever before" (53). Instead of gathering information that would deepen her self-pride, she remembers what will help her to understand the difficulty of obtaining a husband—and relegates her own identity to a secondary role. Roxanne is the first example of "selling the mirror in your soul" or, as Mamie Tilson defined it, "giving up that part of you that lets you know who you are" (59). As Willie and Lester move through this modern equivalent of Hell, Roxanne's story prepares the reader for those that follow, each one with greater degrees of sacrifice.

Lester makes the first attempt to explain this "mirror in your soul" to Willie soon after dinner with his mother and sister. The first reference to the mirror in the book, however, is in the epigraph, a conversation between Lester and his grandmother, where she suggests that selling "that silver mirror" can take a person to hell on earth, every bit as real as the one reserved for the dead. She knows, too, that if Luther Nedeed is not the devil, he is certainly the highest bidder. Lester conveys this explanation to Willie: "So you keep that mirror and when it's crazy *outside,* you look inside and you'll always know exactly where you are and what you are. And you call that peace" (59). Willie hears, but does not understand, Lester; he will need to see for himself examples of those who "sell the mirror."

## David—Winston—(Cassandra)

Winston Alcott's father had been sent some pictures of Winston and David with allegations that these two men were more than friends. After a serious talk with his son, Mr. Alcott, who lives outside of Linden Hills, encourages Winston to consider marriage. Only through marriage can Winston move up in his law firm and down in Linden Hills, from his present address on Second Crescent Drive. In the *Inferno,* the lustful dwell in the second circle, those "carnal sinners, who subject reason to desire."[21] The story that best illustrates this point is that of the great love of Paolo and Francesca. Their eternal bonding in Hell is interpreted variously by critics either as their having conquered Hell or as a part of their punishment. Francesca, married to Paolo's brother, falls in love with Paolo. Francesca's husband catches the lovers in a compromising position and kills them both. They are buried in the same tomb. Francesca tells their story while Paolo weeps; Dante's reaction is to swoon, "as if in death."[22]

The depth of the love these two have for one another is suggested by Naylor in the relationship of Winston and David: "Because when two people still held on like he and David, after all the illusions had died, and accepted the other's lacks and ugliness and irritating rhythms—when they had known the joys of a communion that far outstripped the flesh—they could hardly just be lovers. No, this man gave him his center, but the world had given him no words—and ultimately no way—with which to cherish that" (79–80). And no matter the commitment they feel towards one another, their love can only be seen in the world of Linden Hills as damning. Ready to "sell his mirror," Winston knows marriage is "the only way if a man wants to get somewhere in Linden Hills" because "no one's been able to make it down to Tupelo Drive without a stable life and a family" (75). Winston wants it all—the material status that the marriage will provide *and* David. But David takes the moral high road; he will not be Winston's whore.

The woman Winston will marry is named Cassandra, to whom Naylor gives no words. Her presence only, without language, is an effective way of marginalizing her in a story that is not hers. Along with Winston, she, too, has sold her own mirror to live in a home on Tupelo Drive. The name choice predicts what her future could be, what she might say and not be taken seriously. In Greek legend, Apollo loves Cassandra, but she resists his affections. Though she has the gift of prophecy, Apollo denies her credibility. When she warns the Greeks about the Trojan horse, no one believes her.

Naylor adds a Walt Whitman poem to the wedding, having David use it as his toast in his role as best man. Before reading the poem, Whitman's "Whoever You Are Holding Me Now in Hand," he asks Cassandra to "imagine that [her] new husband is saying these words" (88). Willie, who is listening from the kitchen, knows at once that the poem is by Whitman and is shocked when David changes the *he* to *she*. Willie understands that this poem was written by a man who elevates the love of another man above a woman's love. Willie realizes, then, the strong bond between Winston and David. The poem comes from the "Calamus" section of *Leaves of Grass,* where Whitman treats "manly affection," claiming, according to Gay Wilson Allen, his biographer, "a higher, more unphysical ('disembodied'), satisfying love for a man."[23] There is both an honesty and a cruelty in David's choice of this poem as Whitman speaks for him to Cassandra, wanting her to hear the lines through Winston's mouth: "I give you fair warning . . . I am not what you supposed, but far different." In this room, which lacked spontaneity, where the guests would "be afraid to sweat," and where they all watched "themselves having this type of affair" (83), Willie had noted that Winston's smile looked "like someone had punched him in the stomach and his lips sorta froze up that way" (84). And when David reads the poem, Willie notes that Winston was having trouble breathing and that the earlier smile was replaced by a mouth that "was shaping itself to drink poison" (90). While Lester, operating from his grandmother's perception, appears to take the scene in his stride, Willie articulates the hard questions; he makes the first step towards understanding "making it."

## Xavier Donnell and Maxwell Smyth

Xavier Donnell rolls onto First Crescent Drive in his 1950 Porsche with a horn that plays "God Bless the Child." His destination is Roxanne Tilson, the woman he cannot help falling in love with. The song his horn plays is one of Billie Holiday's hits, first mentioned as a favorite of Etta Mae Johnson in Naylor's first novel. The vague pronoun reference in the lyrics of the line "God bless the child that's got his own" is to money. Xavier, one of two black men on the tenth floor of General Motors, has the money, but he wants something more, and he needs advice from the only mentor he has, the other black man on the tenth floor. Maxwell Smyth, who considers himself not black because he has "spent every waking moment trying to be no color at all" (106), arrives at Xavier's aunt's home, which will be Xavier's when she dies, on Third Crescent Drive because he wants to know "what could be so important that Xavier had to try so hard to make it sound trivial" (107). The corresponding third circle in the *Inferno* is reserved for gluttons, and Maxwell's arrival on Third Crescent calls ironic attention to food and drink. Maxwell has so controlled and minimized his diet that he does not even need toilet paper in his bathroom, except for guests. His consumption has played havoc with his ability to perform sexually, which he does not consider a great deprivation, for Maxwell has spent "his entire life [in] a race against the natural—and he was winning" (104). Maxwell's name is suggestive of the Maxwell demon, a hypothetical agent that admits or blocks passage of individual molecules from one compartment to another. Named for the Scottish physicist, J. C. Maxwell, this agent violates the second law of thermodynamics, the branch of science concerned with the conversion of heat into mechanical energy. Maxwell's body control violates natural laws of human behavior.

Maxwell's encouraging Xavier to forget Roxanne is what

he does not want to hear. Xavier's feelings for her are beyond his ability to understand logically or control sensibly. The language Naylor uses is incestuous yet sexually erotic: "The colors and tints from the thighs *that brought him into the world,* the breasts *that kept him alive and warm.* The mindless plunge and search for the eternal circle that would let him die over and over *in the cavity that gave him life*" (98, emphasis added). He speaks of having come "a long way from the womb" to his position as high priest to "worship the rise of a Super Nigger" (98–99). Carrying this awareness with him day and night, he imposes on himself a reality in which he cannot ever lay down his guard. If Roxanne knows his vulnerability, he will be reminded of a moment from his childhood, one he has no intention of revisiting. The connection of Roxanne with his mother is suggested by her eyes, which are "echoes of those eyes that put ice packs on his bruised genitals when he was sent home early from boy scout camp" (99). The reference to bruised genitals suggests that Xavier was assaulted as a child. It is the embarrassment of having his mother know this and her consideration of his feelings that he replays through Roxanne. His inability to articulate this connection to Roxanne is lived out through his high priest status. If he keeps the shield up, he will never have to be vulnerable again.

During Maxwell's visit with Xavier, Willie and Lester have been cleaning out the Donnells' garage. When they bring their grimy selves into the house to collect their pay, a brief discussion between Maxwell and the young poets ensues, in which Maxwell tries to claim that poverty among blacks need not necessarily be the standard. In order to make his point,

Maxwell brings the four men together over a copy of *Penthouse.* The occasion is the first black woman in the centerfold; she has "one leg raised in victory on the shoulder of a scrawny white man" (115). While the men, at first, "were close and quiet" (115) as they looked at the picture, Willie was quick to withdraw from the others and take offense at Maxwell's demeaning insult: "Today *Penthouse,* my friends, and tomorrow the world" (116). On Third Crescent Drive, Lester simply acknowledges and Willie learns a second lesson about yet another way to "sell the mirror of the soul."

## Lycentia Parker and Chester Parker

Lycentia Parker is dead. She is first mentioned in connection with Nedeed's preparation of her body and the suggestion of licentious catfish head activity on his part. Her name serves as a charactonym once removed in its description of a trait, not of the character herself, but as a response to this character. At the funeral service, Willie witnesses Nedeed closing the lid of her coffin, but he is alarmed and somehow sickened by what he sees, which he thinks was really only "a man leaning over and with his hand closing the lid of a coffin," but, nevertheless, one whose hand "moved too slowly over the top of the lid before it clicked shut" (186). Guided by his father, Nedeed ignored what he had learned in school and worked with the fluids and the right touch to have the deceased female body give herself up "completely to [his] handling" (185). His father had left him alone with his first body after explaining everything but "the contents of the plastic bag on the table" (185). The bag contained the catfish heads, which were inserted in the body in such a way that he received sexual gratification. And from one Luther to the next, this carnal attraction to the dead through the use of catfish heads had been surreptitiously passed on, a means of uniting all the Luthers—without ever saying a word. Nedeed knew he had done his best work with Lycentia. Through Willie, who inadvertently observes, and through Nedeed's own actions, the assumption is clear that Nedeed has gone beyond the bounds of proper morality. Through an omniscient narrator lodged inside Nedeed, he can look "at the results of his labor [which] sent a pleasant sensation through the base of his stomach. She was perfect" (185).

Willie and Lester arrive at the back door of the Parker home on Fourth Crescent Drive to do an unspecified chore for Chester Parker, who is hosting his late wife's wake. This address corresponds to the fourth circle of the *Inferno,* home to those who hoard and those who squander, pushing their respective weights in a circle. Chester is the embodiment, simultaneously, of each as he runs in his own circle trying with expediency to remove the dead Lycentia's personal stamp from her room, becoming almost hysterical (183) in his display of grief at the funeral service, especially when the minister screams Lycentia's name into the coffin. Chester's feelings are ambiguous: her waking, as Lazarus did when Jesus called, is an event that reflects both hoarding and squandering: it would thrill him that she has returned from the dead and would horrify him that he has already prepared for a new wife in her place. He has called Willie and Lester to steam off the old wallpaper full of huge irises (127), a flower that has historical and artistic associations as being sacred to the Virgin Mary. The removal of the irises of Lycentia's wallpaper and the arrival of a chrome vanity set with a white leather seat (129) suggest a Madonna-whore binary relationship that pulls on Chester. Willie and Lester's guesses about the new furniture indicate an intuitive sense of men like Chester—"psychedelic pink with vinyl cushions" or "brass with purple velvet cushions" (129).

Convincing himself by repetition to Willie and Lester, Chester claims that Lycentia would want him to move forward with all due speed. The reader's awareness that Chester does not have the slightest understanding of his deceased wife is made clear when conversation at the wake turns to the approval of the housing project to be located too close to Linden Hills for comfort. Chester's remark that "Lycentia would have wanted it that way" is challenged by guest Bob who knows "she was dead set against it" and that "all that aggravation is probably what killed her" (131).

The talk takes place around a glass-topped table where twelve rotating guests join host Chester, who serves food delivered from a caterer. Naylor's repetition of the number twelve, the continued eating, the shape of the table suggest a mindless Last Supper ritual. Through Willie's vantage point for observation, he responds to another lack of spontaneity, the same dynamic that caught his attention at Winston's wedding. Naylor uses Wallace Stevens' "Cuisine Bourgeoise" to have Willie comment on the perversion of the biblical Last Supper—in "these days of dis-inheritance [people] feast on human heads." As the dinner guests discuss a way to keep out of the neighborhood brown-skinned people who look like themselves, they realize they will have to form a coalition with the Wayne County Citizens Alliance, little more than "the Ku Klux Klan without a southern accent" (134). Simultaneously, the participants at the table devour methodically "the brown and bloody meat" (133). Through Willie's vision, the meal, as the elements of Communion, undergoes a transubstantiation, changing from roast beef into human body parts—"an ear here, a chin there. Parts of a mouth, a set of almond-eyes" (133). Willie's vigil at the banister overlooking the dining room table positions him both to hear the discussion, listen to the "click-scrape" of the communicants, and see the disengagement of people who have lost their internal mirrors. Stevens' poem captures the moment and asks the questions Naylor wants to emphasize through Willie: "Who, then, are they, seated here? / Is the table a mirror in which they sit and look? / Are they men eating reflections of themselves?" (139).[24] Willie's third lesson in "making it" is graphically chilling.

## Rev. Michael T. Hollis

Throughout Naylor's first two novels, Sinai Baptist, staid church home to the wealthy, is contrasted with Canaan Baptist, spirit-filled church home to those people outside of Linden Hills where Mattie Michael from *The Women of Brewster Place* and Willie's family are members. Naylor's choice of names for these churches ties physical geography with their personalities—Canaan, an oasis of promise; Sinai, a desert of dullness. The Rev. Michael T. Hollis serves the Sinai Baptist Church, or, more accurately, with its double balconies, big brass organ pipes, grand piano, comfortable red cushions on the seats, plush carpeting, commanding stained-glass windows (154), the church serves Reverend Hollis. His assignment to Sinai Baptist marks the beginning of his own destruction of that internal mirror. Here he loses contact with his ability to be a medium through which the spirit can flow, and he exchanges his wife for more time with the bottle.

As a youth Hollis had been called to the ministry by being engulfed in the call and response tradition of the African-American church, that "intense flow of energy moving between the pews and the podium" (157). Though later in his life he cannot articulate this exact moment, he seems content to let the calling remain mysterious, knowing only and "simply [that he had] wanted a career in the church" (158). In his childhood conversion moment, Naylor uses Matthew 3:3, "I am the voice of the one crying in the wilderness . . . ," where John the Baptist becomes the incarnation of Isaiah's prophecy, to remind the reader of the irrevocable power of a call. Interspersed throughout Hollis's morning dressing ritual, Naylor accents expensive personal grooming items and merchandise from high-status retailers with italicized lines from Ephesians 6:11, 14–17, 19–20. Read together, these verses from Paul are a commitment to the universal Church: those that belong are called by God, redeemed by Jesus, and incorporated into a fellowship that is sealed by the Holy Spirit. To the church at Ephesus, Paul proclaims the need to be armed with a breastplate of righteousness, shield of faith, and helmet of salvation, for which the church member accepts being "an ambassador in chains."

Hollis has long ago abandoned this biblical call to arms in

order to fight the wiles of the devil. Once, in his grandmother's
world of worship and in the storefront places of South
Philadelphia during his college years, he had found among the
scarred wooden table, plastic crucifix, and battered piano, "that
type of raw power [that] connected up with something in his
center" (159). He has exchanged that power for his Linden
Hills address. Paul's letter to the Ephesians is also a reminder
of the importance of the Trinity, but Hollis's use of the Trinity
has become a cheap way to explain to Willie and Lester his
address, 000 Fifth Crescent Drive: "Three eternal circles that
are quite appropriate for a home owned by the church. . . . Yes,
the holy trinity. Each having no beginning and no end. I wanted
that as a reminder to the community—and myself—that there
are so many forces that govern our lives beyond the material,
the tangible" (169). But Hollis speaks with a forked tongue, for
he has chosen his address to answer Nedeed's, 999 Tupelo
Drive: "Luther Nedeed might see himself as the omega, but
Reverend Michael T. Hollis was the alpha" (165). Hollis's reference to himself as the beginning suggests his developing
grand illusions, for, in reality, his alpha does not extend beyond
Linden Hills.

On the morning of Lycentia Parker's funeral, Reverend
Hollis has a hangover, which he attempts to cure by the-hair-
of-the-dog method. That same morning, Willie and Lester
arrive at his home on Fifth Crescent Drive to load and then
deliver the decorations and food for the annual Sinai Christmas
party. Dante pays the sole tribute to his mother in the fifth circle. Willie, likewise, remembers his mother in relationship to
that Sinai Christmas party she had taken him to throughout his

childhood. In retrospect, Willie focuses on his mother's feelings for the first time, "how she must have felt taking [Willie and his siblings] to that party each year and having to sit in those pews," when the family was so poor that their "one hundred percent could barely clothe" them (155). Willie knew there was no ten percent to tithe to any church, and suggests it would have made no difference at Sinai. Willie's strong powers of observation, heightened by a childhood with an alcoholic father, provide Willie with a revised view of Hollis and with his fourth lesson in the shattering of the internal mirror.

When Willie thanks Reverend Hollis for those Christmas parties of his youth, Hollis takes their exchange to heart. Fortified with the liquor in his blood, he preaches a sending off for Lycentia that Sinai Baptist has not heard in thirty years. Hollis's passionate performance echoes the message Moreland Woods wooed Etta Mae Johnson with in *The Women of Brewster Place*. With the solitary help of one soprano, who puts her everything into "Amazing Grace," and then follows with the old African-American response to the preacher's call, a stunned Sinai Baptist hears only Lycentia's husband, Chester Parker, join the soloist in responding. In this sole attempt to reclaim the power that had brought him to a life in the church, Hollis sees that Luther Nedeed's calm delivery of the eulogy restores the comfort level to a neighborhood not used to feeling any emotion. Rather than embracing the lifeline of that power, Hollis chooses deliberately to crush it and win back his church. All the words of Paul to the church at Ephesus about fighting the devil's wiles in this world are inverted in this moment. Luther, as devil, has won another round, so when Hollis returns to the pulpit, he does "absolutely nothing in those final moments but intone the words: 'Let us rise. And pray'" (184), and his victory is a Pyrrhic one.

## Laurel Dumont

At 722 Tupelo Drive various members of the Dumont family have been in residence for over sixty years; Laurel has been there but ten. The address corresponds to the seventh circle of Dante's Hell, the site of violence to others, to the self, and to God. In Canto XIII, Dante and Virgil visit this place where suicides are punished. At 722, a suicide takes place as Laurel Dumont chooses a final dive during the coldest time of the year. Willie is the first to discover Laurel's body; he is summoned to the back yard by the sound of an impatient voice that could easily be "the cry of an old woman, calling a little girl home" (216). Naylor links each of the plaintive repetitious calls of Roberta Johnson, Laurel's grandmother, with memories which prepare the reader for a retrospective trip through Laurel's early days—the connection with Roberta in her Georgia backwoods country home and Laurel's early obsessions with water and music. But what Willie sees—"a tall, slender body in a silver bathing suit crushed into the bottom of the empty pool" (216)—is a sharp contrast to the innocence of the sounds of her grandmother's pleas.

All Willie sees is the end of Laurel, but what the reader learns is the story of her childhood. Told through Roberta's point of view, this all-giving grandparent constantly placed the child's welfare above her own. When she thought of Laurel going under the water and not returning to the surface, she knew that "no power on earth could have kept her on that shore, and she didn't swim a lick" (219). When Laurel complained about not being allowed to cut her hair, Roberta had brought in the heavy weight of the Bible and was willing to misquote it in order to support Laurel's father's position: "Besides, the Good Book says that a woman's hair is her crowning glory" (222). The Bible is without mention of crowning glory, but the closest reference to these words is Proverbs 16:31, a reference to an aging man, "A hoary head is a crown of glory; it is gained in a righteous life." When Laurel's father denied her the money to attend Berkeley, Roberta cashed in her life insurance to make that dream possible. During the whole of her life, Laurel had but to ask, to hint, to whine, and Roberta made it happen. Because the locus of the telling is placed in Roberta, Laurel's early years have but three key components: Roberta herself, music, and water.

Laurel's visits with Roberta in her childhood summers are filled with time spent in the water and developing an interest in classical music—ultimately combining to become the music that Laurel hears while in the water: "It's like there's no difference between the air and the water except that the water is safer" (224). Through Laurel's increasing need to be in the water where the music exists "if you knew how to listen" (224), Naylor suggests Laurel's desire to return to the womb. Her mother has died too early. When Laurel is upset, she sinks to repeating her wistful cry: "I want my mother. I want my mother" (223). After Laurel graduates from Berkeley, her passion for water and music is supplanted by a stifling career in business, an up-and-coming district attorney husband, and a home in the lower region of Linden Hills. Roberta cannot grasp the depth of Laurel's growing despair, and Laurel herself is horror-stricken when she realizes she is "imprisoned within a chain of photographs and a life that had no point" (228).

Naylor calls attention to Laurel's absence from Roberta's life by using language that negates the positive, for at Roberta's home there were "uneaten dinners kept warm on the back burners" and "freshly made beds not slept in" (229). When Laurel finally does arrive, the questions she asks—"Well, can I come in?," "And can I give you a hug?," and "Aren't you glad to see me?"—are just three stupid questions to Roberta (229). Laurel has abandoned her feelings, forgotten what she should know in her heart; she has sold out in order to toil uncomfortably in false material pursuits. Roberta lives in her feelings, so when she tries to help her granddaughter, the language she speaks emanates from a different origin. Laurel's return to Georgia that summer because she thought that "when people are in trouble . . . they go home" (231) puzzled Roberta because she knew that a Georgia shack is not home, but merely a place where she had hoped Laurel "had learned to be at home with [herself]" (236). For Roberta, home is portable; for Laurel, home never becomes more than a house with a prestigious address in Linden Hills.

When the two move from spoken language to music, the classical music that has been the heart of Laurel's world is strange territory for Roberta. Her musical world is Bessie Smith, Billie Holiday, and Muddy Waters—singers and musicians that epitomize the blues. Roberta is baffled by Gustav

Mahler's work, a man whose music she claims "ain't made peace with his pain" (235). The tape that Laurel subjects her grandmother to in the last weeks of her life runs the gamut from a young Brahms to the last symphony that Mahler composed. The mood of the music runs consistently downhill. The music of Laurel's morning choices—Rachmaninoff, Beethoven, and Brahms—is more optimistic and livelier than the afternoon music—Chopin, Tchaikovsky, and Mahler. A more somber finale would be difficult to name, but the discussion between Laurel and Roberta that comes as a result of listening to Laurel's music choices together is temporarily hopeful. However, Laurel's inability to reach Luther's wife by phone, Ruth's canceling her visit because she is not feeling well, and Luther's ominous visit in which he informs Laurel that her husband has filed for divorce and is going to let 722 Tupelo revert to its original owner—all combine to put Laurel over the edge on the 23rd of December. In her final dive, Laurel manages to perform all three of the violences for which people are punished in Dante's seventh circle—violence to others, the self, and God.

Willie's response to his fifth lesson in "internal mirror destruction" is visceral. He is not privy to Laurel's story. Because he is the first to see the body, his release of "lumps of yellowish-green mucus" into the snow (249) is uncontrollable and natural. When he discovers that Luther Nedeed has stood and watched Laurel take the dive, his sense of sickening horror immobilizes him. An old teacher, surprising him, appears and offers hospitality. Here in the seventh circle of Hell, one story runs into another, as Braithwaite's appearance from just one street down (251) would put him in the eighth circle, home to the hypocrites in Dante's world. When Braithwaite refers to Laurel Dumont as Howard's wife, Willie has to correct him, to name her. Three times he states the name: "Laurel. . . . Laurel. . . . Laurel" (252). Willie may not know her story, but he will defend, after the fact, her presence that was in the world.

## Dr. Daniel Braithwaite

Daniel Braithwaite has been watching Willie and Lester all week from his clear vantage point through a huge double Plexiglas window, which permits a view all the way up to the rooftops of First Crescent Drive. When Laurel Dumont takes her fatal plunge, he is instantly there to offer warmth and wisdom to Willie and Lester. He is a retired history professor whose life's work has been chronicling the history of Linden Hills. His address, one street down from 722, in Dante's corresponding eighth circle suggests a connection with hypocrisy. From his perspective, however, he has seen the first Luther's dream be tarnished by people whose interest in black power has been substituted by a mindless notion that moving into and down in Linden Hills is "the thing to do, the place to be" (260); this is spoken by a man who appears to value his own prestigious address. Braithwaite is convinced that the original tenants understood that, in an oppressive white world, here in Linden Hills "there was something to strive for, something to believe in" (259). Willie and Lester, on the other hand, see a fraud because he had chosen not to do "*something* to keep the steam down" (257) in the case of Laurel Dumont. When Lester starts to quote his grandmother to Braithwaite, he knows the line about "selling the mirror" so well that he finishes it for Lester. Braithwaite believes the opposite of Mamie Tilson: these people have not sold anything. Rather, he thinks they have had it taken away (260) and that Mamie has "mistook the ends for the means" (261). Braithwaite has lived too long and seen too much. Luther Nedeed distributed the first six volumes of his 12–volume history to the residents of Linden Hills. All the information they needed to understand the "record of a people who are lost" was in their hands, but Braithwaite is certain no one ever bothered to read it.

The choices Naylor has made for the library in Braithwaite's house are key volumes for any historian interested in black history. The *Crisis,* the official journal for the NAACP, began in November 1910. The *Journal of Negro Education,* started in April 1932 at Howard University, and the *Journal of Negro History,* with Carter G. Woodson as editor, began in January 1916, while *Black Enterprise,* a later journal, began chronicling the African-American involvement in business in August 1970. The *Atlanta University Studies* are published reports of annual conferences held on this campus in Georgia beginning in 1896. For about the first twenty years, W. E. B. Du Bois was the chief organizer, and the topics varied yearly but always emphasized the African-American's position within the topic. Examples include economic cooperation, morals and manners, the college-bred, and the Negro American family. The first edition that Braithwaite owns of W. E. B. Du Bois's *Philadelphia Negro* dates to 1899, and the other named volumes, in chronological order, include Booker T. Washington's 1907 *The Negro in Business,* Carter Woodson's 1934 *The*

*Negro Professional and the Community*—a book that is part of the effort of The Association for the Study of Negro Life and History to explore and trace their social and economic conditions—and Edward Franklin Frazier's 1962 *Black Bourgeoisie.* The thick volume of *Poetry of the Negro* (255) is most likely Langston Hughes and Arna Bontemps's anthology of poems from 1746–1949, which first appeared in 1949 in 429 pages and was revised in 1970 and extended to 645 pages. The one specific poetry collection Braithwaite names is Countee Cullen's 1929 *The Black Christ.* Cullen, along with Hughes and Bontemps, were the most widely acclaimed poets of the Harlem Renaissance. Other critics have associated Naylor's name choice with William Stanley Braithwaite (1878–1962), a poet who never revealed his race in his published poems.[25] This position is a troublesome one because many others viewed this historical Braithwaite as hostile and ashamed of his race, while he saw his position as a small sacrifice in order to do more quantitative good for his race. Another name source is a man with the same name that Naylor has chosen, the author of the 1956 *The Banning of the Book* Little Black Sambo *from the Toronto Public Schools.*

The fictional Braithwaite believes his duty stops with recording the information; he does not feel morally compelled to do anything beyond that. Willie meets his comment with the first line of the fifth stanza of T. S. Eliot's "Gerontion": "After such knowledge, what forgiveness?" but will not say from whose poem the line comes. Braithwaite's world—in his library, in his work, and in his neighborhood—is an all-black one. Willie's refusal to name the white poet, contradicting his

earlier insistence that Laurel be called by her name, is excused
in his mind as a courtesy to Braithwaite: "You don't repay
kindness with needless cruelty" (263). Naylor's use of Eliot's
poem in this story suggests that Willie is the boy who reads to
the old man in a decayed house. The poem includes references
to wars he never fought and history with its "many cunning
passages." Once Willie and Lester learn that the gnarled willow
trees are dead and that dead trees, in Braithwaite's mind, assist
his work, Willie's interpretation coincides with Eliot's words:
"To lose beauty in terror, terror in inquisition" (264). For
Willie, this sixth lesson is the most personal. Braithwaite
remains a hypocrite to Willie because he knows what he does,
but he chooses to be powerless to affect change. Willie believes
that Braithwaite has a responsibility to do something with what
he knows, but Willie has not yet learned to transfer this lesson
to his own life.

## All the Mrs. Luther Nedeeds

"Her name was Willa Prescott Nedeed" (277), but the
reader does not know this information until her twelfth appearance in, and near the end of, the novel. Through the fifth
Luther's wife, her story, along with three other Mrs. Luther
Nedeeds', is told. Naylor's placement of each of the fifteen
segments of the stories of the Luthers' spouses is deliberate—
reflecting and commenting externally on the story that is
unfolding for Willie and Lester and internally on the story that
is unfolding for Willa. The fifth Luther manages to get his wife
and son down to the old morgue in his basement where he has

provided two small cots, rigged a rough means to deliver her water, all to provide her with time to "think about what she'd done" (20). He has decided that her son cannot possibly be his because he is not the right color: "He looked at this whiteness and saw the destruction of five generations" (18). Luther operates out of the logical manner of reasoning he has been taught by his father; no Nedeed wife has ever had an influence on, a presence with, or a name remembered by her husband or her son.

In different typeface, through Willa, Naylor creates space for the rest of the story to be told. And it begins with a long, thin howl (42) that reverberates up and out of Linden Hills and into the Andersons' apartment on the night Willie and Lester are visiting, is reduced to something weird (47) by Willie en route to Lester's home, and becomes a long, thin wail that shoots through the slightly open window in Lester's bedroom. The final mention of what must be Willa's response to her son's death is unacknowledged in the world and returns for Willa alone to handle—back through the brick pillars, back across the frozen lake, and down through a basement air vent (61). With as much despair as appears in the book, Willa swallows her own sounds, her own rage, for that wail will "die in the aching throat of a woman who was crouching over the shrunken body of her son" (61). She will have to find her own way out, and her story cannot begin until the unanswered wail has boomeranged.

The novel does not include explanations of how Luther manages to relocate his wife and son to the basement and how the sixth Luther dies. Willa's story begins with her reactions after both events have happened. First, every fiber of her being is connected to the dead son she clutches to her chest as she waits for her own death to follow. As the water flows into the basement, a slow disconnection with the corpse begins, and Willa knows that "Luther was a dead man if she left that basement alive" (71). Willa's dream of "pale women wrapped in lace bridal veils" (90) who dance around her cot appears to be the impetus to separate physically the body of her son from her body. Realizing that "grief was only attached to memories," she had to put her dead son into "the cradle of her mind" (91), so she could remember him and begin the grieving process. Naylor uses abstract language to evoke concrete images: "the thought [sits] in her lap and she stare[s] at it" (91). This segment of Willa's story appears during Winston's wedding, connecting those lace bridal veils from her dream with the wedding that is happening simultaneously in Linden Hills. While her husband is making his presentation to the newlyweds of a home on Tupelo Drive, she is wrapping her dead son in the actual lace bridal veil of the wife of the first Luther, the young boy's great-great-great grandmother.

Bridal veils become the medium through which enormous sacrifice is symbolized in the present and in the past. For up in Linden Hills, Winston forfeits the man he loves for a woman, and down in Linden Hills, Willa wraps her dead child and inadvertently learns the story of Luwana Packerville's past sacrifice—each event laced to the other by the bridal veil. The origin of the bridal veil includes opposing tales, for the veil has been cast as both an emblem of freedom and a sign of submission. Most fitting here, however, is the bridal veil's history as a shroud, worn first on the wedding day and then used again on the occasion of death.[26] As the day of Winston's wedding draws to a close, Willa's mourning for her son begins.

The next day, as Willie and Lester, beside Xavier and Maxwell, lean over *Penthouse*'s first black centerfold, Willa leans over Luwana Packerville's Bible. In their different yet respective ways, Willie and Willa are both seeking to understand a mystery. For Willie, it is wondering if that exposed woman "with her dark face, full lips, and high cheekbones [who] was a dead ringer for his baby sister" (116) is, in fact, his sister. For Willa, the story of the woman who is her ancestor-in-law unfolds slowly as Willa discovers Luwana's letters and reads them on a literal surface level, stunned by a distant story of loneliness that matches her own. But the texture of that loneliness deepens if readers understand that the various placements of the letters between specific books of the Bible expands their meaning.

The ancient biblical stories are the backdrop for and the means by which Luwana in isolation creates a second self. Through the public act of writing down her own story, she makes contact, though over a century has lapsed, with a woman who follows too closely in her path. Luwana's despair over discovering that she is still a slave and the humiliation that her owner is also her husband falls between the books of Jeremiah and Lamentations. Luwana's rage at her "cursed bondage" (117) echoes Jeremiah's consistent protest against political policies while Lamentations is an expression of grief for generalized sorrow that incorporates an appeal for divine mercy. What must be Luwana's first entry—the only one of hope, for she is leaving the South, with rejoicing and looking forward to "a new land. A new life" (118)—is placed between Genesis and Exodus. The first book of the Bible, Genesis, is the story of beginnings, and Exodus continues the message of the first book, while emphasizing the central event of the Hebrew Bible, the escape of the slaves from Egypt into the wilderness en route to Sinai. The optimism of the ancient slaves parallels the hopes of those people held in slavery during the early years of United States history, as the years in the wilderness reflect what Luwana, upon this writing, had yet to discover.

The rules about housekeeping (118) are placed in Leviticus, a book devoted to delivering the proper procedures for ritual sacrifices and ritual purity. Luwana's sadness about not knowing her own mother is another way of saying that she was sold from her before she could remember her. That story is placed by Ruth, another motherless woman who chooses to cleave to her mother-in-law Naomi after both their husbands are dead, to abandon her own Moab for Bethlehem, willing to let Naomi's people, land, and lifestyle become her own. Particularly ironic is the fact that the first Luther has no known mother; it is as though he sprang full grown into his created world of Linden Hills. The fears she records of becoming a new bride are placed by Song of Solomon, a book containing the most erotic themes of human love, with lush, extravagant imagery and appeals to all senses. Just as the Luthers are meant to be portrayed as a continuum, Willa knows from other men she had been intimate with before her marriage that "it could be—should be—different from this" (148). So, too, she knows that Luwana's fear, whatever it might have been, must have

*LINDEN HILLS*

soon dissipated into a fear that that kind of passion would never be hers to know.

Between First and Second Kings, Luwana has placed the story of Luther's manumission of her son, which includes her full realization that she will be owned by him. The book of Kings continues the story from the book of Samuel chronicling biblical history from the time of the Judges to the Exile. All the kings were judged on the basis of religious loyalty, with David as the standard, whose death is recorded at the beginning of First Kings. Naylor's placement of Luwana's story in this location highlights the increasing awareness that this character has of how women's way in the world is subjected to the ongoing control of men; the emphasis in First Kings on men's power in the world, passing from one to another, is a line that moves through hundreds of years.

When next she records her feelings, they appear in the New Testament, for "four hundred years of proclamations by these iron men of God" (119) left her no solace and no room to tell her own story. Naylor makes clear to the reader that Luwana has no community that awaits word from her, so the placement of her loneliness in Acts and Romans is appropriate. Luke, the generally acknowledged writer of Acts, records the advance of the gospel from Jerusalem to Rome. Paul, who wrote letters to the people of Rome, encourages early congregations not to lose their faith. Luwana explains her isolation and creates a second self, a sister with her same name, the self she was back home in Tupelo, Mississippi, in order to have a feeling, as Paul surely had, that somewhere in the world there was someone waiting to hear from her. Biblical scholars know

that Paul's letters were often in response to questions or concerns he was asked by the people, but the Bible does not record
those letters. The southern Luwana, controlled by the Linden
Hills Luwana, does write back to remind her of the "devil she
knew" as a slave woman, the endless annoyances that Mistress
Packerville barraged her with daily: "And she would even call
you from the pantry while your hands were smeared with
dough to hand her a thimble that was barely two feet away"
(122). The "devil she knew" becomes child's play next to the
"devil she didn't know" until she went north with Luther.
Luwana's last entry meticulously records the number of times
in a year she has been called on to speak. She arrives at the
number 665, and knows that on the next day she will possibly
be called on to say goodbye to her son who is leaving for college and "that will be the 666th time that [she] will be called
upon to open [her] mouth" (124). This number names the
Antichrist from the book of Revelations, who, finally, is all the
Luthers.

While Willie observes the guests eating at Lycentia
Parker's wake, Willa opens a cookbook in her basement con-
finement. Searching for further word from Luwana, she meets
instead another predecessor, Evelyn Creton Nedeed, who,
according to the dates, was the wife of the third Luther Nedeed,
the Luther about whom the least is known. As Evelyn's story
unfolds for Willa, she sees a person obsessed with cooking, one
who "baked continually and in equally huge amounts" (140).
The recipe books—"two slim volumes covered in black silk"
(141)—divulged her secrets. Willie's dream after overeating
the food Chester Parker sent home with him speaks to him,

demanding, "Willie, eat it . . ." (145), is echoed by Willa's questioning, "Will he eat it?" (147). As Willa pours over the list of ingredients in Evelyn's recipes, she notices the addition of dove's heart, amaranth seeds, snakeroot—products from nature that would draw a positive force from Luther. Had Willa listened to her great-aunt Miranda Day, her reading of these additions would be more knowledgeable. Naylor's inclusion of the central character of her third novel, *Mama Day,* appears at this point, and only in Willa's memory of her own more youthful days. Had she listened to Mama Day's advice—"Child, y'all sittin' there complainin' 'bout them wayward boys. Ain't never seen an onery man yet who didn't come round if you get yo'self a little shame-weed and bake it up in somethin' sweet" (148)—or had Mama Day visited once in the six years she had been with Luther, then the story would have taken a different direction, for the Mama Day that may yet have not been fully developed in Naylor's mind would have seen this man's evil ways.

In the midst of the funeral for Lycentia Parker, Willa's thoughts give the reader a more nearly full explanation of Luther's attraction to catfish heads. Through her thoughts, Willie's concern about Luther's attention to the body takes on deeper significance. Willa wants to place what she saw in a dream, for if it had not been "she couldn't have kept living with the man she saw in the mortuary that evening" (174). When she followed him to his work that night, she claims to have run "from guilt, not from the sight of him lifting a fish head out of a plastic bag and turning it gently in his hands before inserting it in the spread body before him" (175).

Willa notices the differences in the two stories; while
Luwana's deprivations and sorrows were hers alone to bear,
Evelyn's cooking moved forward in an intrusive fashion. First,
there was an attempt to win her Luther over through nature's
wonders, then Evelyn's ingredients displayed her desire to conjure control over Luther—the menstrual blood of virgins, the
genital hair, dried bull's testicles (188)—and Willa knows that
Evelyn must have lived with the hope that he would never
notice what was happening to him. Since Evelyn cooked so
much, Willa determines she must have been immense (189),
but then notices that laxatives in enormous quantities make
their way to her lists. Abandoning hope of affecting Luther in
either way, Evelyn determines to torture herself through the
intake of these purgatives. Finally, it is the prussic acid (191)
that Evelyn uses to take her life, most likely mixed in the
vanilla ice cream that the delivery boy brings on Christmas
Eve. This distant suicide foreshadows the one that will happen
at 722 Tupelo, to Willa's only friend in Linden Hills, Laurel
Dumont.

Willa's discovery of the pictures leads to her third and
final Mrs. Nedeed, Priscilla McGuire, who happens to be her
mother-in-law, the fifth Luther's mother, her child's grandmother. Naylor does not acknowledge that Willa knows this
fact. Through the pictures that Willa kicks about the basement,
having determined that all these women were insane, one face,
she feels, says to her, "I knew you would come, and I'm so
pleased to meet you" (205). That face, however, begins to disappear through the annual family portraits over the years, until
finally a convergence on three levels occurs in the novel—

Willie's dream of buying his mother a Disc camera but being told by the saleswoman that he has no face (211), Willie's, "without thinking, he turned [Laurel Dumont's body] over" (249), and Willa's comment in the next sentence, "Her face was gone" (249). Priscilla's absence in the family culminates in the last photograph where only an empty hole exists in her place and in "lilac-colored ink was the word *me*" (249).

After encounters with these three Mrs. Nedeeds before her, Willa has to decide if she still exists. Above, Willie, afraid to sleep lest he dream again, begins work on his 666th poem: "There is a man in a house at the bottom of a hill. And his wife has no name," which leads directly to Willa's story where her name is stated, the first step to knowing that she did exist. The review of her own life comes full circle to her having walked down the twelve steps into that basement and her determination now that she was prepared to walk up those same steps and back into her home. The number twelve that Naylor chooses for the number of steps corresponds to the famous 12–step recovery programs for those who are trying to overcome addiction. Willa's first step on the climb upward corresponds exactly with Willie's accidental opening of the metal bolt that Luther had used to lock Willa out of her home. As the Christmas boxes he balances there tap against the bolt on the door, Willa, miraculously, opens the door from the other side. Her presence startles Luther, and he scurries to get Lester and Willie out of his house, to deal with the dead child, and to determine what he perceives as Willa's insanity. In the confusion, a fire consumes the three of them—Luther, Willa, and their already dead child. Willie, who wants to do something (300), and Lester, who wants to get out of there, are helpless and can only watch the fire burn. Willie, who earlier, chastised Dr. Braithwaite because he did not do something, now understands the feeling.

Traitors dwell in the ninth circle of Dante's Hell, and this is the home of Luther Nedeed. The frozen lake Cocytus has its counterpart on the frozen lake from where Willie and Lester watch the fire burn. Satan is depicted as having three faces, and when the three charred bodies are brought from the ruins, it was as "one massive bulk" (303). As Dante is led out of Hell by Virgil, so Lester leads Willie out, suggesting the best way to depart. Willie's deepening lessons about the internal mirror that must not be lost, sold, forgotten, or broken are reflected in the somewhat psychic bond he holds with Willa, who in order to leave that basement must first be able to see herself in some external mirror, to know that she still exists. The structure of the novel is an external and internal mirroring—reflecting externally Dante's *Inferno,* some of America's greatest poets, books of the Bible, contemporary African-American writers, and finally, internally, Willie and Willa.

# CHAPTER FOUR

# *Mama Day*

The title of the 1988 novel makes no reference to geography. From *The Women of Brewster Place* to *Linden Hills,* Naylor's choice of *Mama Day* directs the reader's attention immediately to a character and suggests that a specific place will assume subordinate importance. Unlike the cover art of the first two novels, which did little to suggest any significance about either the titles or the substance of the books, the artwork on *Mama Day* begins the exposition of the title. Both the first edition cloth and the succeeding paperback editions carry an artist's depiction of two black female hands coming out of the tops of trees, reaching towards the heavens, with lightning either emanating from one of the hands into the unknown at the top of the book or coming from the unknown down to the hand. Either reading of the lightning's origin still makes the hands enigmatically larger than life. These are not ordinary hands; therefore, this Mama Day must be no ordinary woman. All this is clear before the reader opens the book. Maybe.

In addition to the front matter found in any book—the title page, the copyright information, the dedication page—the book also contains a two-page unidentified map. On the left hand side is a roughly drawn picture of where South Carolina meets Georgia. On the right-hand side, an island is placed in the Atlantic Ocean, although a fence runs underneath the island and through the ocean. The island has a plump lima bean shape with one Main Road and assorted houses and stores. On the map, the title character's home is a trailer beside a chicken coop. This is the home of the character first introduced in *Linden Hills,* Willa Prescott Nedeed's great aunt, Miranda Day, the relative Willa was so ashamed of, the one who came to visit "with her cardboard suitcases, loose-fitting shoes, and sticky jars of canned whatever. Toothless but ready with a broad grin; almost illiterate but determined to give her very loud opinion regardless of the subject or the company."[1] Following the map is a page repeating only the title, *Mama Day.* The reader connects those powerful hands on the cover with someone who lives in a trailer. Are the hands really Mama Day's hands?

A genealogical chart depicts Mama Day's relatives, all descending from one Sapphira Wade, who is shown on the chart as being the sole life giver to seven sons. The seventh son gives birth to seven sons. The seventh son then gives birth to three daughters, the eldest being Mama Day. Her middle sister gives birth to three daughters, whose second two daughters each have a daughter. The next page posts a bill of sale replica, dated 3 August 1819. Bascombe Wade purchases a "negress answering to the name Sapphira. . . . suspicious of delving in witchcraft."[2] On the next page, words finally appear, and the beginning is "Willow Springs" (3), the first mention of the specific place that is characteristic of each of Naylor's novels. Narrative prose, however, is not the beginning of this book, and it is essential that the reader remember this point in order to embrace the world view that Naylor creates in this highly original, magical masterpiece. Before the reader arrives at this page, contradictions and puzzles through cover art, map, chart, and facsimile lay the groundwork for this novel.

The first eight pages of prose are an introduction to the novel. A voice speaks to the reader, one who is unnamed but dwells among those who live on Willow Springs. The reader is introduced to the legend of Sapphira Wade and, depending on who is talking, this woman can "grab a bolt of lightning in the palm of her hand" (3). Back to the cover again. This line suggests that the hands must be Sapphira Wade's, not Mama Day's. Everything the reader needs to know about the important events of the novel is delivered in these introductory pages. However, because the reader is quickly immersed in this new world where a story needs to be told to the stranger-reader about a subject that exists in the nonverbal part of memory, readers find themselves rereading, returning to the earlier pictorial display, and eventually trusting that language, which does not make logical sense, will eventually do so. The reader's naïve hope is that the book will come around. Naylor's gift to the reader is that she ushers in a world which must be accepted on its own terms; the reader is the one who must come around and learn to experience a world in which, as Hamlet declared, "there are more things in heaven and earth, Horatio, than are dreamt of in your philosophy" (I.5.166–67).

Naylor prods the reader gently throughout the introduction, as one living Cocoa and one George, dead and buried on Willow Springs, "talk about that summer fourteen years ago when she left, but he stayed" (10) without either of them saying a word. The reader is part of the picture, as though a guest, alongside Reema's boy, who has been tainted by "those fancy colleges mainside" (7) and has forgotten what he knows, having grown up on Willow Springs—that its people do not communicate with words. The reader-outsider must listen and come to know in ways that exist without verbal explanation, by "shelling June peas, quieting the midnight cough of a baby, taking apart the engine of a car" (10). Willow Springs takes the reader into the numinous world, where understanding comes through the mysterious, the ethereal, and permeates the whole self. To know through the mind is insufficient and secondary to sensuous saturation.

Because of the striking difference in the two worlds Naylor builds, one beside the other—one, logical and rational; the other, unpredictable and otherworldly—contemporary reviewers are often perplexed. Missy Kubitschek claims that these reviewers have "mistaken its genre and defined its originating traditions too narrowly," and that they have missed the two basic characteristics of African-American culture: "the past's persistence in the present, the present's participation in myth and archetype."[3] Every southerner understands the former component—that the past is always present, but the latter point is especially important for understanding moments in the novel that elude the reader's grasp. Faith Pullin sees the "collision of those two worlds provok[ing] tragedy," with "a narrative swing from myth to social realism," but concludes that the island is "outside time and is the setting for a tale of melodrama and intrigue." Melodrama is always associated with exaggeration, an overstatement of emotion; the word choice is pejorative and confusing in a review where Pullin concludes that the work is "funny and entertaining; evocative and powerful."[4] Likewise, Laurence Hull seems confused by a moment for which his language stretches to sum up a pivotal point too easily: "[the novel] is marred by the unintentionally comic death of a major character, who is attacked by a vicious chicken."[5] Hull's grasp does not go into myth; he has not heeded the initial narrator's direction to listen. It is not the chicken's attack that kills George, but rather his unwillingness to have listened, really listened to Mama Day's instructions. George's death following the chicken scene gave other reviewers a challenge; Patricia Olson sees this "central salvific event" as not making sense, but she adds, "even in terms of the symbolic world of Willow Springs."[6]

Although parallels to Shakespeare are obvious, according to one reviewer,[7] few choose to expand on these connections. Bharati Mukherjee enumerates a short list, mentioning the novel's roots in *The Tempest* and a reference to George and Cocoa as star-crossed lovers (*Romeo and Juliet*). Furthermore, Cocoa's real name is Ophelia, Hamlet's erstwhile love interest. Mukherjee also suggests that the courting of the lovers is similar to Kate and Petruchio in *Taming of the Shrew.* Ultimately, Mukherjee does not like the two lovers, labeling Cocoa shallow and self-centered and George priggish. She is, however, willing to embrace Naylor's creation of alternate realities.[8] Rosellen Brown, on the other hand, thinks George is "as sympathetic as any man to appear in the recent fiction of black women."[9] And Martha Southgate, writing for *Village Voice,* likes him so much that by novel's end she wanted to marry him.[10] While Shakespeare dominates the text in allusions, reviewers have pointed out links with Alice Walker, Toni Morrison, Zora Neale Hurston, and Charles Chestnutt's *The Conjure Woman.*

*Mama Day* is a novel that takes place in four worlds—first

on Willow Springs (without Mama Day), a mythical island, which does not exist on any map, but has a history rich and mysterious; in New York City where Cocoa and George meet and fall in love; in Willow Springs (with Mama Day) where Mama Day and her sister Abigail, Cocoa's grandmother, have always made their home; and, finally, in Willow Springs as the two worlds come together when George, representative of the "now," visits the island where everything that ever was is also now. The structure of the novel takes its shape out of the history and way of life and death that is the heritage of Willow Springs.

## Willow Springs: before/without/through/beyond Mama Day

In Naylor's first two novels, place experiences a birth ritual. Both Brewster Place and Linden Hills are conceived and given life by and through men. While Willow Springs had long been in the family holdings of the Norwegian Bascombe Wade, having been claimed by the Vikings during their days of exploration, its existence apart from the United States makes no difference until it is deeded to the offspring of Sapphira Wade. Everything that matters about Willow Springs finds its source in the legend of Sapphira Wade. Depending on which unknown, unnamed voice is talking, Sapphira is either black, cream, or red, with power to heal by using the moon as salve and the stars as swaddling cloth. Nothing about Sapphira is related in human proportions. According to the bill of sale, African-born Sapphira was sold in August 1819 to Bascombe

Wade. Four years later in 1823, at the age of 24, depending on who is talking, the following reports circulated, each more fantastic than the other: Sapphira either smothered Wade, poisoned him, or put a dagger through his kidney; she married him; she either bore him (or someone else) seven sons in a thousand days; she persuaded him to deed the island to those seven sons. The narrative spokesperson for Willow Springs, the introduction's tour guide, knows that the only "wild card in all this is the thousand days" (3), for according to the genealogical chart, Sapphira gives birth to seven sons in six deliveries. In the best of circumstances and of good health, it would take almost twice a thousand days to accomplish this. There is no way to know and no way to explain for "Sapphira Wade don't live in the part of our memory we can use to form words" (4).

Naylor gives those seven sons names from the Old Testament. Their biblical counterparts are all associated with activities or feats that defy logical comprehension: Elijah and Elisha, who appear together in I and II Kings, with Elisha, remembered as a miracle worker, being the successor and disciple of Elijah, who ascended into heaven in a fiery chariot; Joel, the second of the minor prophets in whose book a plague of locusts is predicted; Daniel, who interprets dreams and is miraculously preserved during his time in the lions' den; Joshua, who succeeded Moses and led Israel's conquest of Canaan; Amos, a minor prophet whose book contains vision reports and prophecies of both conflict and resolution; and Jonah, another of the minor prophets who is best remembered for fleeing in the direction opposite to which God wanted him to go and for experiencing conversion in the mouth of a whale. Their last name is not

Wade, but rather Day because Sapphira, taking her lead from God who rested on the seventh day, did the same and chose that word for the family name.

Because 1823 was the year associated with all the possibilities of Sapphira's activities, "18 & 23" becomes a metonymy on Willow Springs for a "way of saying something" (7). When these numbers are placed in varying contexts, they mean whatever the speaker wants them to mean. Even though the use of "18 & 23" is private in-speak for Willow Springs' inhabitants, the reader has no trouble substituting a meaning within the greater context of its usage. When a would-be suitor comes knocking at a girl's back fence and the mother responds with "Get your bow-legged self 'way from my fence, Johnny Blue. Won't be no 'early 18 & 23's' coming here for me to rock" (4), the context clearly portrays the mother's lack of interest in rocking any babies. Other uses for 18 & 23, which can be any part of speech, demonstrated by the tour guide as noun, verb, and adjective, show its wide applicability: hormonal surges, sexual desire, cheat, troublesome, something worth doing, love. Naylor has the tour guide stress the absurdity of trying to make sense out of the expression by using Reema's boy as the representative of "across the bridge thinking." When this former resident of Willow Springs returns to do his field research for a book he is writing, he turns 18 & 23 into 81 & 32, "which just so happened to be the lines of longitude and latitude marking off where Willow Springs sits on the map. And we were just so damned dumb that we turned the whole thing around" (8). In the introduction Naylor impresses upon the reader, sometimes overtly and at other times more subtly, the attitude with which the book should be read: it is not important to twist every odd quirk that lacks credibility into logical meaning. The schools only teach one way of learning and that way can "turn our children into raving lunatics" (8). Willow Springs offers alternatives.

Reema's unnamed boy is used as a model by which the reader learns how not to behave on Willow Springs. Had he gone to see Mama Day and Abigail, he would have heard a story; he would have learned how to quench his thirst with a few sprigs of mint; and he would have known to put moss inside his shoes before he stepped foot in the graveyard. He would have heard the story that is the novel itself. All this is conditional for Reema's boy; he does not do the things necessary to hear the story. Mama Day might as well not even be on the island. Had he paid attention when nobody was talking, he could have come to see how Candle Walk and the standing forth have shaped the island's people. The reader is to learn from his mistakes, or the reader will not come any closer than Reema's boy to understanding *Mama Day*.

### Candle Walk

Candle Walk night is held each year on December 22. Through the years, its manner of celebration has evolved, but it remains a time when people give to other people "any bit of something, as long as it [comes] from the earth and the work of your own hands" (110). Its origin is associated with aspects of the Sapphira Wade legend—the one about God spitting out the island along with an array of stars, which, when God reached to retrieve them, He "found Himself shaking hands with the greatest conjure woman on earth. 'Leave 'em here, Lord,' she said. 'I ain't got nothing but these poor black hands to guide my people, but I can lead on with light'" (110). Mama Day's father, John-Paul, knew from his childhood that people "kinda worshipped his grandmother, a slave woman who *took* her freedom in 1823" (111). Legend has it that she walked down the main road, "candle held high to light her way to the east bluff over the ocean," in order to journey back home to Africa in a ball of fire (111). Later, people lined the road during this annual occasion to help her spirit along (111). Her departure in a ball of fire back across the ocean suggests a reference to the folktale of the flying Africans. In any number of ways, the slaves, tired and worn out or seeing little promise in their future in the American South, made their way back to Africa.

Historically, the countries along the western coast of Africa were the areas from which slave ships picked up Africans and made the passage across the Atlantic Ocean, often stopping in Haiti or the West Indies. These people brought with them from their motherland a strong sense of their religion and their magic. Slave owners were more fearful of their slaves congregating in groups to practice their religious rituals than they were of their involvement in more solitary activity; practicing alone, the medicine men and the conjurers had opportunity to flourish. Medicine men were practitioners of good magic, while conjurers were more likely to use their powers for more harmful purposes. The large number of slave revolts has been attributed to the presence of these people because the slaves had an assurance of supernatural support and a promise of ancestral aid in their fight for freedom.[11] Conjurers were secretive about their sources of power, and it was usually not the case that someone could master these skills by studying; rather, conjuring was an inherited craft.[12] Knowing that Sapphira Wade is "the greatest conjure woman on earth" and that she inherited this wisdom suggests the importance of her African ancestral heritage; that the ability to conjure is inherited indicates Mama Day's and Cocoa's lineage as well.

Naylor uses the Candle Walk ceremony to let the reader know that any certainty is fragile. For when Mama Day ends her Candle Walk, as she always has done, in the East Woods, facing Africa, she learns something she had never before considered. The legend has it that Sapphira murdered her possible husband/confirmed owner, but only after conjuring him into deeding the whole of Willow Springs to her offspring. However, on this Candle Walk night, Mama Day sees differently as she enters her usual space: "A long wool skirt passing. Heavy leather boots. And the humming—humming of some lost and ancient song. Quiet tears start rolling down Miranda's face. Oh, precious Jesus, the light wasn't for her—it was for him. The tombstone out by Chevy's Pass. How long did he search for her? Up and down this path. . . . Up and down this path, somehow, a man dies from a broken heart" (118). The map reminds the reader that Bascombe Wade is buried on the side of the island facing Africa, just south of the East Woods, and if indeed the light was not for Sapphira, but for Bascombe, to aid his searching, a whole new interpretation of that relationship comes into possibility—that Bascombe was not conjured, but gave the island willingly and out of his love for Sapphira. Nay-

lor's choice of present tense for her concluding statement—
"somehow, a man dies from a broken heart"—places Bascombe's past demise in the present, but it also projects into the
future and predicts that George will follow suit, for in this
place, George, too, will die from a broken heart. This collapsing of time suggests that, on Willow Springs, all that was and
will be can be understood in the all-present now.

### Standing Forth

Just as there is no Christmas on Willow Springs, there are
no funerals, although George wants to call it that, this ceremo-
nial ritual for the death of Little Chick, the much-beloved son
of Bernice and Ambush. Those rebuilding the bridge after the
great storm suddenly stopped working and announced: "It's
time to go to the standing forth" (268), a collective impulse
which has its roots in a much earlier period. Those who are
native to Willow Springs do not bother to explain anything to
George, the outsider. He first marvels that the group halted
work abruptly without a signal. The trappings of Judeo-
Christian funerals—flowers, music, a manner of dress, tears—
are all absent in the Willow Springs standing forth. The time is
determined in a way which seems mystical to the outsider: people interrupt whatever activity they are involved in and walk
toward the church—a towel wrapped around freshly sham-
pooed hair, in a beauty parlor smock, a house coat, fuzzy slip-
pers, dirty overalls. As death interrupts life without warning, so
does the standing forth interrupt life's routines, catching people
in all stages of public readiness.

The event takes place in the church and the minister is present, but his role is marginalized, reduced to less than a master of ceremony: "Charles Kyle Duvall, 1981 to 1985. Who is ready to stand forth?" (268). He then sits down and only intermittently repeats, "Who is ready to stand forth?" The standing forth narrative is delivered through George's voice, and the reader learns along with him because George is the novel's character who most closely resembles the reader's world view. His surprise at what he experiences at the standing forth is honest; what he thinks surely will not happen, does happen. Bernice and Ambush do not wear black or special clothes. One at a time, person after person, as each one prepares to speak, he or she walks to the front of the church, looks down at the closed small coffin and begins with these important words: "When I first saw you . . . ," followed by a recollection of the first meeting and closes with "And when I see you again. . . ." (268), followed by an extension of that first recollection. For example, "if they first saw him walking, they would see him running" (268). No voice breaks in the standing forth, but George knows the parents cannot possibly offer their words in this public forum because Ambush's grief could be "cut with a knife" and Bernice "had gone out of her mind when that child died" (269). Naylor slowly develops her use of dramatic irony: the reader, at this point in George's visit to Willow Springs, knows that when George says something will not happen, it will. Ambush, first, and finally Bernice have their standing forth moments, and while their voices are low and quiet, they do not cry. No official words conclude the standing forth—only a community's recollection of individuals beginning the relationship with the promise that at some later moment in time that relationship will pick up again.

The standing forth is a brief moment in the entire book; however, Naylor uses the standing forth as her means of structuring the whole novel. The reader is not aware that all of this book is a standing forth until Little Chick's death ceremony, which is neatly contained within several pages close to the end of the novel. Early on, the unnamed voice of Willow Springs who speaks directly to the reader in the introduction prepares the reader for the story that Reema's boy would have heard if he had only known how to listen. The next page begins the story of George and Cocoa in New York. Through alternating voices, they tell their shared story.

The reader could easily forget that George is dead and that Cocoa is alive. She sits by his grave and talks to him without words; from the grave, he talks back to her without words. Cocoa, the living one, has the first say, and her say, the first of twenty-eight, begins with her recollection of the first time she sees him, the very beginning of the relationship that is to come. Her sentence begins as though to complete "When I first saw you," the unspoken standing forth prompt: "You were picking your teeth with a plastic straw . . ." (13). True to their relationship, though, George must participate as well, telling his own side in his thirty-four turns, correcting her, recollecting the beginning of his relationship with Cocoa. So it continues for the next several hundred pages, the whole of their days in New York and then the whole of their time together in Willow Springs, his one and only visit during that event-laden summer of 1985, when Cocoa left, and he stayed (9). And as it should be near novel's end, Cocoa has the last word, for she is alive, so she concludes her standing forth for George, this time with the prompt spoken: "But when I see you again, our versions will be different still" (311). From here, Naylor returns the reader to that unnamed voice on Willow Springs, who, like Cocoa, has twenty-eight opportunities for contributing to the story's development. The epilogue simply continues the introduction; the intervening pages have been an interruption, a necessary diversion because Reema's boy did not know how to listen. The year is still 1999; Mama Day is preparing to die, but first she wants to "tie up the twentieth century" and "take a little peek into the other side" (312) of the next century. Her conjuring powers from the great, grand Mother, Sapphira Wade, also now reside in Cocoa. So Mama Day is free to go, ready "for a rest that she deserves" (312).

## New York City, with George and Cocoa

When Ophelia (Cocoa) Day recollects the first time she saw George Andrews, she takes the reader to a coffee shop on Third Avenue in New York City and unwittingly draws a picture of her earlier self, shallow and bigoted. People become foods—cherry vanilla, fudge cream, licorice, kumquat, a whole Baskin-Robbins, bagels, and spareribs. Even George is a fudge stick, while her new boss is a rump roast. In the only honest question that matters on their first date, George asks Cocoa, "Why are people food to you? . . . Stuff you chew up in your mouth until it's slimy and then leave behind as shit the next day" (62). Cocoa is forced to make a chink in the wall of defenses that she has constructed over the seven years she has lived in New York. For her, home in Willow Springs is utterly predictable—nothing changes and "when you saw a catfish, you called it a catfish" (22). Cocoa's bombast is a feeble effort to hide her screaming insecurities; she reasons it is her "way of coming to terms with never knowing what to expect from anything or anybody" (63). George helps Cocoa to see that she is failing miserably in her efforts to assess New York and its people, trying to read her choice of places to live as she thinks she must rather than bringing to this environment her real Willow Springs self.

In the early days before they begin the relationship, Cocoa shows a sense of the woman she will become when she applies what her grandmother and great aunt have taught her: "living without manners in this world is not living at all" (58). When she calls George to thank him for the flowers, he pauses, and her response, as though it is somehow other controlled, paints a small moment by which the reader's gaze may also be directed in looking at this relationship: "In just that half a breath, the caring in your silence stunned me. . . . It was like when a kid labors over a package—the wrapping paper is poorly glued, the ribbon is half tied—and all of his attention is directed toward that space between the hands that offer and the hands poised to receive. It's the gesture that holds the heart of the child" (59). In keeping the focus between George and Cocoa on what is always about to happen, in the pregnant moments of potential, the reader experiences the development of the relationship along with both of them, not favoring one's position over the other. In this gesture, Naylor also calls attention to hands, hands that are about to connect, yet frozen in the space of this moment. Throughout the novel, Naylor places emphasis on the power of hands that do connect; finally, it is George's inability to understand what he is to do with his hands that contributes to his death.

From the beginning, George's position on life is clear. From the days of his childhood at the Wallace P. Andrews Shelter for Boys, the source of his last name, his guardian, the shelter director Mrs. Jackson, has impressed upon him, "Only the present has potential, *sir*" (23). George has been taught to depend on himself alone. His world is one of "only rules and facts" (24). Yet from the first meeting with Cocoa, she is dangerous to his way of thinking precisely because she makes him not think. The first striking contrast between the two would-be lovers is their views of time. For Cocoa, the rich history of her own past and its active involvement in her present clashes with George's insistence on now.

The story which best illustrates why George, as an adult, insists on the now has its roots in the tale of the mysterious disappearance of the sodomist whom Mrs. Jackson and her helper Chip caught in the act and took away to her place. She never called the police, as she said she would, and the next day Chip dug a new rose garden. The wheels of justice crank slowly and Mrs. Jackson obviously had no second thoughts about determining this lowlife's stay on earth. The boys who wondered were told only to "keep it in the now, fellas" (25). This illustration is packed with too much emotional baggage for a young boy's mind—why would someone do that to boys under eight? Why would Mrs. Jackson say she would call the police? Did she, and they did not come? What happened to the man? Was he dead? Was she responsible for his death? For a boy, this is too big to handle—keeping it in the now is a means of survival. Those boys "had a more than forgettable past and no future that was guaranteed" (26).

At the end of their first summer together, Cocoa accepts George's offer to see his New York, and while they are busy doing what George would have done by himself, and summer turns into fall, the two mutually yet hesitantly fall in love with each other. For Cocoa, "nothing [she] had met in that world had prepared [her] for [his] possibility" (99), and for George, he "woke up one morning, sometime in early November, and realized [he] wanted to be with [her] for the rest of [his] life" (123). The mutual intensity of feeling is disturbed by what almost doomed the relationship—the richness of Cocoa's family heritage against George's isolated status as an orphan. He is eager to hear about her life on Willow Springs, about her being raised by her grandmother and great aunt; she is willing to pour out the stories, for she is merely an extension of that heritage. But George is reluctant to share what he has been told of his past because he has been taught by the shelter rules to keep it always in the now. Cocoa thought his silence had to do with an inability to share his feelings; she believed that everybody knew "a person is made up of much more than the 'now'" (127).

When Cocoa goes to visit an old boy friend and George waits outside the building all night for her, he greets her with a slap the following morning. Naylor recalls this moment with

Cocoa's mouth: "And your voice was matter of fact when you took your hand out of your pocket and slapped the living daylights out of me" (130). Cocoa's memory of this physical outburst places no blame on George, for she contextualizes the slap within George's finally telling his own story—that his mother was a whore (with the immediate suggestion that Cocoa had just behaved as one) and that is why he abhors being called a son of a bitch; that he was born in a brownstone near Bailey's Café in Harlem; and that his mother's body had washed up against the pier at 125th Street. George gives a report surrounded with mystery: "Later, her body washed up down there. I don't have all the pieces. But there are enough of them to lead me to believe that she was not a bitch" (131). In the telling, George has walked Cocoa to these places on 125th Street, and as he finishes his tale with what kind of son he had been, she listens to his story with her eyes closed. As Cocoa has learned from growing up on Willow Springs, really listening involves more than looking at somebody and hearing what he says; rather it has more to do with absorbing the story through all the senses.

George is the one who uses the term "star crossed" (129) from *Romeo and Juliet* to describe their relationship, but, defying rational thinking, the way in which she listens leads her to propose to him. Though much of the courtship of George and Cocoa has been a fairy tale romance, a genre in which the two would get married and live happily ever after, the wedding ceremony is reduced to a report. Naylor chooses to skip the ceremony's details and move to a post-wedding announcement through an unnamed voice on Willow Springs: "Down the road at the Days' there's busy preparation for a miracle that Miranda says has already happened: Cocoa's marriage" (135).

New York is George's hometown, and like his beloved King Lear, he reigns supreme over his kingdom, knowing how to divide it into territories, visit its various sections, and show them off. Like Lear, he wants verbal affirmation from Cocoa that she sees them his way, that for her people cease to be food groups but rather individuals with stories worth knowing. George might not be asking Cocoa the question that Lear asks his daughters, "Which of you shall we say doth love us most?" (I.1.50), but he wants Cocoa to see his city his way. George attributes his fondness for *King Lear* to a special poignancy which he feels when he reads "about the rage of a bastard son, [his] own father having disappeared long before [he] was born" (106). The vicious Edmund, however, is no parallel to George. When he is not the lord of his New York kingdom, he is more like the good Kent, who encourages Lear to "see better" (I.1.157) because that message fits George's aim for Cocoa. As George responds kindly to Cocoa's relatives, he also comes closer to being like the legitimate son Edgar, who, disguised as Poor Tom, aids his blind father Gloucester. George may claim he feels the rage of Edmund, but in Shakespeare's character that rage is directed toward evil deeds, which is never the case with George.

Further, New York is Naylor's representation of the locus of rational thought, what Willow Springs people would call "across the bridge thinking," a pejorative term meant to reflect a narrow and shallow comprehension of the world's ways. The absurd potential in this kind of thinking is demonstrated when George tries to understand his new wife by reading books about how women's bodies work, and discovering that women "were normal only about seventy-two hours out of each month" (141). When the wedding quilt arrives the first summer, George wants to "clear a wall in the living room and hang it up," while Cocoa knows that the quilt was made to be used, and not just for her and George, but for Cocoa's "grandchildren to be conceived under this quilt" (147).

Finally, when the time comes, after four years, for George to join Cocoa on her annual trip to Willow Springs, he plans with his typical rational preparation, only to be thwarted by the discovery that Willow Springs is not on any map. And this omission "upset [George's] normal agenda" (174). Trivial to Cocoa and seriously important to George were questions for which he could find no answers: "What county claimed [Willow Springs]? Where was the nearest interstate highway, the nearest byroad?" (174). Naylor's use of synesthesia, the first slight crack in George's rational thinking, occurs when he crosses that bridge into Willow Springs: "My nose and mouth were coated with the various shades of greens, browns, and golds in the muddy flatlands. And if someone had asked me about the fragrance from the whisperings of the palmettos, or the distant rush of the surf, I would have said that it all smelled like forever" (175). This is not New York George talking, but Naylor's point is to show that, while George can leave the city, it is ultimately impossible for the city to leave George. For Cocoa and George, differences too big to overcome are their perceptions of and approaches to time (past vs. present), family ("living mirrors" (48) vs. orphan), and thought (Willow Springs' ways vs. rational).

## Contemporary Willow Springs, without George

Naylor uses only one paragraph to establish that Mama Day reads, sees, and knows the world differently from those who live across the bridge. A drop of vapor from her morning tea turning gold against the carved apricot leaf of her cabinets delivers the message to Mama Day that Cocoa will be "coming in today, a little earlier than expected—and on the airplane to boot" (34). This introduction is followed by Mama Day's need to watch the *Phil Donahue Show* on television because the people who comprise the audience are from Chicago; in Mama Day's mind all big cities are the same, so reading the eyes of that television audience helps her to understand New York, Cocoa's world. Even without the sound turned up, Mama Day knows who gave up "their babies for adoption, which fathers have daughters making pornographic movies, exactly which homes been shattered by Vietnam, drugs, or 'the alarming rise of divorce'" (38). The fact that Cocoa is confident that Dr. Buzzard will be there to meet her plane even though she does not let her grandmother and her great aunt know the details of her arrival are clues for the reader, who approaches this section of the novel with the same inability to listen that Reema's boy demonstrated. Mama Day's powers on this mystical island are a reminder of the legacy that Shakespeare's Prospero might have taught Miranda in *The Tempest*. Her response to Buzzard is similar to Prospero's attitude towards Caliban. Mama Day rebukes him for his small trick of hiding Cocoa on his truck behind the jars of honey with a lacerating sting: "nothing human could have put you on this earth" (46). Mama Day's response to Buzzard, a con artist who claims to be a "hoodoo doctor," appears hyperbolic.

From the time Miranda was five years old and had to comfort her younger sister Abigail at the death of their other sister, Peace, Miranda has understood "there is more to be known behind what the eyes can see" (36). Naylor chooses this early moment in the characters' lives to explain the intimacy of the sisters' connection; as Miranda crawls into the bed to offer physical comfort to her little sister, "they are four arms and legs, two heads, one heartbeat" (36). The year is 1900; the connection continues for the next 90 years, and even after Abigail's death in 1990, the ritual greeting between the two continues in some form: "No need to cross that road anymore, so [Mama Day] turns her face up into the warm air—You there, Sister?—to listen for the rustling of the trees" (312). Abigail's line, "Uh, huh," is handled by and through the sounds of nature. By novel's end, the reader is not surprised by Mama Day's ability to read her environment because through the course of events, she has taught the reader how to "listen. Really listen" (10). When Mama Day picks up the phone to call her sister, who lives across the road, to report that Cocoa will be coming on the afternoon of the day she gets the message through the vapor from her tea, Abigail's response assumes Mama Day's knowing—without concern for origin of the information. She has, after all, been aware of her sister's powers for almost eighty years.

Mama Day is the oldest daughter of John-Paul, the seventh son of a seventh son. John-Paul and Ophelia give birth to Miranda, Abigail, and Peace, the last of whom meets an early death when she drowns in a well, an event which contributes to Ophelia's madness. Events surrounding Peace's death mark the recorded moment in the novel when Miranda comes to understand there is more to know "behind what the eyes can see." For when there is no Peace, there is also no peace—the search for which is a major drive in all the Day women. Abigail names the first of her three daughters Peace, in an effort to restore peace to the family, but, even though Mama Day begged (39) Abigail not to do so, she would not listen; the child "didn't live long enough to get a crib name" (39). A crib name is a nickname given by the "mama's mama," a name that responds to demonstrated traits of the baby. Abigail's second daughter, Grace, gave birth to Ophelia, who received a crib name that connected her beginning with the great, grand Mother of them all, Sapphira Wade, and young Ophelia became "*the* baby girl," who at five "refused to answer to Baby Girl. . . . So they gave her the pet name Cocoa" (39). Abigail's last daughter is Hope, whose child is Willa Prescott, the one who dies in a fire in Linden Hills, recounted in gruesome detail in Naylor's second novel. Looking at Willa's wedding picture, which Hope had sent Mama Day and Abigail shortly before her own death, Mama Day had only to take one look at Luther Nedeed to know that "there's more to that Christmas Eve fire than meets the eye—much more" (39). Cocoa, the child of Grace/grace, is the "only one left alive in this generation to keep the Days going" (39).

Naylor uses every event on Willow Springs to establish for the reader that Mama Day has magical powers that have become commonplace to its inhabitants. Everybody on Willow Springs knows and fears Mama Day—she delivered a good number of them—and these local people listen when Mama Day talks. When white strangers appear in their midst, like the new deputy that comes over from across the bridge to find the maker of moonshine, he sees only "an old colored lady with a bag of groceries and a red straw hat cocked on her head" (80) correcting his language. He has to be shown who is in charge on a night that just happened to have one of its worst lightning storms in a decade (80). Because the storm is without rain or wind, with only lightning bolts burning the air, Naylor suggests that Mama Day is connected with the origins of this convenient storm. When she refuses to take Cocoa's friend Bernice to the other place to assist her in having a baby and sends her home with instructions to be patient in the wait for a baby, she trusts Bernice will listen to her. But when she discovers that Bernice wants fertility drugs and has plans to seek help from Dr. Buzzard, Mama Day threatens Buzzard in such a way that he knows better than to respond to Bernice. When husband Ambush summons Mama Day to their house one evening because Bernice is on fire with fever and may lose the baby (70), she already knows that Bernice is not pregnant. In the act of gathering eggs to make cakes for Cocoa's visit only several weeks earlier, Mama Day reads each of the eggs she draws out from her chickens. With a lighted candle, she searches for clear, firm yolks (41). A blood spot or a sign of life being formed indicate the egg is not one she can use. When she gets the eggs into the house and breaks them for cake making, she reads the yolks. The first yolk tells her that Bernice will not conceive a baby that next month; the following two yolks indicate the same report for the following two months. The role of chickens and their eggs, introduced here, takes on significant importance in the eventual birth of Bernice's son and later in George's death.

When Mama Day, in the act of diagnosing Bernice's infected ovary, sees how much effort Bernice has put into the nursery for a child she wants so dearly, she offers a plan to make Bernice strong and a promise to go to the other place if necessary. By the time Mama Day returns home, she understands what "the air was telling her. She knew now for certain that her and Bernice would end up at the other place" (91). The other place is the birthplace of all the Day offspring, but it is also the place where sister Peace drowned in the well, and Miranda and Abigail's mother went crazy, sitting in her rocking chair twisting pieces of thread until the day she "flew off that bluff screaming Peace" (117), and "John-Paul and three of his brothers dragged the bottom of The Sound for a week" (117), never finding the body. Since that time, Abigail would not go to the other place. Mama Day explained to Bernice that, whatever happened, there would be a secret; even Ambush could not be told. From the moment the night air spoke to Mama Day, she realized that what had to be done there was going to be "tricky though, real tricky" (91). Mama Day knew also that the young pullets she saw in her back yard would be right come spring, but she would have to "take [a box of them] out to the other place" (91). Naylor repeats the reminder to the reader twice on the same page—she could take the young chickens to the other place, but "the rest was gonna be tricky, real tricky" (91).

Bernice's preparation for pregnancy during the fall and winter is directed by Mama Day. Because Mama Day's history of delivering babies, healing sicknesses, and strengthening weaknesses is a matter of public record, the reader has to pay careful attention to each of Mama Day's moves regarding Bernice. First, Mama Day takes old equipment from the other place to Bernice's house for her to use; thus she establishes through Bernice—and the chickens that have been taken to the other place—a link with the past. Mama Day's plan for Bernice in the seasons before spring consists of hard work, doing things the old way so that Bernice's body will become stronger, and she will be too tired to realize the passage of time. Bernice's busyness actually allows her even more time, time to sew by hand a dress for Abigail, who declares she will pass into eternity wearing it. Bernice and Ambush—and Mama Day—wait for spring. When it arrives, Ambush becomes a minor player, for Bernice's readiness occurs without him.

In four paragraphs that can easily confound the reader, in Faulkner-like prose, Naylor spins out the scenario of Bernice and Mama Day at the other place. Bernice's preparation for conception via Mama Day and a chicken's egg warrant careful explication (139–40). When the first new moon of spring arrives, Mama Day waits for Bernice in a rocking chair on the front porch of the other place. The rocking chair is either the one her mother rocked in while twisting the piece of thread, because that chair would link Mama Day to the past, or the rocking chair Ambush has meticulously hand carved for her for Candle Walk, for that chair, with its disturbing water lilies, is connected both to Ambush, who will be the father of this child, and to the past as a reminder of sad memories. Either rocking chair would serve Naylor's need to represent the past physically.

Naylor casts the conception scene by using disembodied parts. First, Mama Day and the chicken in her lap become "two pair of eyes waiting and rocking, both unblinking" (139). Mama Day hums "a music born before words. . . . begun in eternity," a suggestion that Mama Day's powers connect to a past that is outside of logical understanding. Bernice is never referred to by name, but rather as she "rounds the bend," she has become a walking embodiment of hope (139). This hope can both taste fear and be reduced to only feet walking as hope changes into fear when she enters a garden "where flowers can be made to sing and trees to fly" (139). The other place is no ordinary place. But fear can revert to hope when she finds "a voice: Mama—Mama Day?" (139).

The humming, older than time, and the rhythmic rocking and stroking of the chicken contribute to its laying an egg, but Bernice, who now has become confusion waits too long to eat the egg, which grows cold "under the hidden moon" (139). The chicken's eyes do not blink, but Mama Day's eyes frown as she smashes the egg onto the porch steps (139). Bernice personifies silent (139) as she waits for the chicken to produce another egg and for Mama Day to pass it her way. As knowing (139), she takes the wet egg, breaks it, and eats it. Every poultry farmer knows that chickens lay one egg a day, but this is the other place, where flowers sing and trees fly, so a single chicken can easily produce more than two eggs in a short span of time.

As Mama Day and Bernice move from the front porch into the dining room, Bernice knows that the white-sheeted dining table has been prepared for her. She takes off her clothes and reclines on the table, feet propped in "the scooped top of each [padded] board" (140). Naylor catalogs the nine openings of a woman's body—five above the neck, two breasts "for the life she longs to nurse," and two below the waist. With her legs spread wide open, Bernice feels the touch of feathers from the chicken that is held by Mama Day's ancient fingers, which keep the chicken's opening and Bernice's in line, so that the chicken's egg—"pulsing and alive"—can enter Bernice, who closes, her body sucking it in from "a rhythm older than woman [which] draws it in and holds it tight" (140). For the extraordinary chicken, this is a third egg, but the reader has stopped counting. If Mama Day is viewed as a mediator, her work is completed. Ambush has but to fertilize this chicken egg with his sperm; Mama Day's part in the preparation for his participation is a secret he will never know. To think that Ambush has a viable part in his wife's conception, however, veers towards a logical rendering of Bernice's pregnancy—and that would be "across the bridge thinking." Ambush's name could well be a play on his own ambush by Mama Day and Bernice. At the other place, it easily follows that chicken's eggs are all that are necessary to create the child that Bernice will carry—both swallowed through separate openings on a woman's body.

Since Cocoa's fight for life as an infant, Mama Day and Abigail have believed that this last-of-the-Days' offspring is

the recipient of powers from Sapphira, but they have never told
her the family story. On Cocoa's first mid-August visit home
without George after her marriage to him and with her friend
Bernice pregnant, Mama Day finds a way to get Cocoa to the
graveyard and to the other place. As the two work to clean off
the tombstones, the narrative voice of Willow Springs tells the
reader the ancestors' stories, who one at a time, as their respective stones are cleared, speak in first person. The reader—who
throughout is being taught to listen, really listen—hears what
Cocoa will learn the way natives of Willow Springs learn
everything they know—without words. As the two arrive at the
other place, Mama Day, using her walking stick as Prospero
used his staff on Shakespeare's magical island, through a wave
and a thump of that stick makes flowers fly and sing. She
speaks to Cocoa, but through her eyes, just as she had spoken
to Bernice the night of her impregnation; they were "ancient
eyes, sad and tired: it's time you knew. An old house with a big
garden. And it's seen its share of pain" (152). Naylor has
Mama Day's eyes address Cocoa directly and she gives the
house the ability to see as well. Cocoa is no longer Baby Girl;
the old matriarch realizes that if peace is ever to settle on this
family, Cocoa must begin to understand her own history. The
history degree she pursues in her northern university is incon-
sequential beside the Willow Springs' stories she must begin to
interpret.

## Contemporary Willow Springs, with George

During the preparation for George and Cocoa's arrival in
Willow Springs, after four summers of Cocoa's coming with-

out George, Mama Day has a particularly harried morning. In fact, she sums up her self-image of what will greet George's eyes: "a beat-up old woman with buttons missing on her dress, runs in her stockings, and a no-'count pair of shoes" (170). She has burns on her left wrist from letting the hot cake pan slip out of her hands. What she thinks must be jitters about George's arrival is replaced by her sudden realization that, while she has never seen George, she does know him; he "ain't no stranger" (170), so when she begins to clean herself, her home, and her yard, she finds a tangible something that the reader must attribute to the morning's mishaps. Neighbor Ruby has placed in Mama Day's yard a hex, which Clarissa, Mama Day's favorite old black hen, has located through her scratching. Convictions about magic brought over from West Africa included the belief that a "frizzled hen kept in the yard would scratch up and destroy all conjures."[13] The flannel that contains the ingredients looks new and Mama Day remembers that the verbena is also called herb of grace and connects that language with Cocoa, the child of Grace (172), who is arriving that day. She remembers a past summer when Cocoa had ridden in the same car with Junior Lee, the totally undesirable man Ruby had conjured away from Frances, whom she drove crazy with her spells. Next to Mama Day, Ruby is a rank amateur, but just so Ruby would know that she knew the source of Clarissa's discovery, Mama Day returns the flannel and its contents to Ruby's yard. Their talk of peaches had nothing whatsoever to do with Mama Day's visit, and in the Willow Springs way, as readers are coming to understand, not a word about the real reason Mama Day was there had to be said. Ruby could see the "grayish dust and purple flowers spilling out around the foot of the gate" (172). Mama Day is rabid about the care of her own, and George, before she lays an eye on him, is included in that circle. Before she would countenance Ruby's conjuring, she would "wrap [her] up in tissue paper and send [her] straight to hell" (173).

When the moment comes for George to meet Cocoa's grandmother and great-aunt, Naylor arranges outward awkwardness to meet inner integrity. Abigail places her hands on each side of George's face and gives him the welcome that melts his engineer-reserve: "well, bless your heart, child," for "up until that moment, no woman had ever called [him] her child" (176). When Cocoa moves to the plural pronoun— "relax, we're coming home" (176)—George, who has not yet been instructed as the reader has, enters the palpable love circle in which Cocoa's roots run deep. This love reaches out to include him, and what he had said the first time he ever spoke to Mama Day on the phone—"[Cocoa] has all I have" (136)— is now going to be true for him. Willow Springs is the place where George encounters reciprocity, for he has all Cocoa has. However, in lessons of the heart, George is not the ideal student; his resistance to surrender logical thought to the ways of Willow Springs costs him his life. In the day-to-day, he refuses to learn the rules of Willow Springs poker, bridge building, and cleaning out a chicken coop. In the mystical realm, he ignores his dreams and Cocoa's descriptions of her illness. George lives in a world that must and can be tested, measured, proven; he values empirical data above all. And this position is his undoing.

The first night in Willow Springs tests George's confidence. He knows New York, but this island eludes him—the silence keeps him awake at night, and even with the comfort of Cocoa beside him, he feels intensely alone (183). His dream during that first night serves as a warning: he is swimming across the sound towards Cocoa's voice but the more he tries to reach her, the more impossible it is to do so. When Mama Day tells him to get up and walk, and he uses his last bit of strength to scream at her about her craziness, he finds himself "standing up in the middle of The Sound" (184). This scene is the reader's first clue that George is a Christ figure in this novel—for walking on water is associated with Jesus. Though he is thirty-five when he dies, not thirty-three, George gives his life for Cocoa.[14] Even though George wakes refreshed the next morning, he does not heed the lesson of the dream, which is so clearly stated: Listen, really listen to and do what Mama Day says. On that same night, Cocoa, lying beside him, has the same dream, only Mama Day's message is not in her version. She knows only to keep quiet, for George's efforts to reach her send him in the opposite direction. She knows she must shut her mouth with her "voice pushing inside [her] chest until it felt like [she] would explode" (189); in her dream, she was useless in assisting George to help her.

Starting the next morning, George, who may be expected not to listen to Mama Day in his dream, begins to practice not listening to her in waking moments. Even though the island calls up for him "old, old memories" (184) and the unused air is "more than pure, it was primal" (185), he still cannot accept what Mama Day says to him. Belittling her folk remedies by declaring that those ways are a current fad in New York, accepting Buzzard's word that he and Mama Day have a professional rivalry, and assuming that he can win at poker, George will not hear what is said to him and repeated by others on the island. This city boy, lover of Shakespeare, who knows *King Lear* so well, never bothers to make the obvious comparison with *The Tempest*'s magical isle and its Miranda. Buzzard is her Caliban and the adjectives she injects into the air about him—"shiftless, no-good, slew-footed, twisted-mouthed, slimy-backed" (191)—add to an ongoing invective she carries for him. Mama Day, Ambush, and all the fellows at the barber shop tell George the rules of the poker game—the goal is to try not to lose too much. George knows only one poker game, with the goal being to win as much as possible. All the voices mean nothing to him; Willow Springs poker with Buzzard has different rules. And when George turns the tide of the evening by winning, he appears to be indifferent to the others' responses, whose fun has been taken away by this outside usurper.

Before Mama Day hears George's name, when he was just someone with whom Cocoa was seeing New York, she learns that he will die, but she reads the message retrospectively only and not as a prophecy. On Candle Walk night, Mama Day goes out by Chevy's Pass, and it occurs to her that Bascombe Wade died from a broken heart, but Naylor's language can be read forward in time as well: "Up and down this path, somehow, a man dies from a broken heart" (118). When Cocoa and George walk through the family graveyard, Cocoa hears the whispers, "all in the wind as it moved through the trees and stirred up dust along the ground" (223), but to those silent whispers she wanted to ask, "how would I break his heart?" (223). Cocoa

# *MAMA DAY*

refuses to accept their message, telling herself she had not heard it. At the other place, the message repeated itself through her great-grandmother Ophelia's rocking chair, *"you'll break his heart"* (224). Then while cooking, Mama Day "feels death all around her" (226), and when she begins to listen, "the pictures move backward and it falls into place" (227). The simple pronoun *it*, without a clear referent, is Mama Day's certain knowledge that George will die.

George had come home from that poker game drunk, and Cocoa knew that her relatives would take it upon themselves to see that George had plenty to keep him busy from that point on. Mama Day had a list of chores, some involving contact with chickens. When she asks him to paint her chicken coop, he does not want to admit that he was a little afraid of live chickens (221). The storm that comes, "an 18 & 23er" (228), briefly interrupts George's connection to and involvement with the chickens, but when Mama Day sends him from the other place to that same coop after the storm and in the midst of Cocoa's fight for her life, George's will, his "across the bridge thinking," his out-and-out resistance to heeding the literal language of Mama Day, results in his own death. Naylor's delivery of George's mission, like Bernice's conception, is puzzling—and serves as a final exam for the reader. For if the reader has learned to listen, really listen, then George's death can be accepted on its own terms, Willow Springs' terms. Mama Day and Abigail both know that George will "do anything in the world for [Cocoa]" (267), but neither one of them was talking about this world at all (268).

That storm is the storm of Shakespeare's *Tempest.* In its

aftermath, Little Chick, beloved son of Bernice and Ambush, is dead. The bridge is destroyed and must be rebuilt by the Willow Springs' inhabitants, who have no interest in listening to engineer George suggest a better way to do it. And unbeknown to Cocoa, Ruby weaves poisonous nightshade berries into her hair. But Cocoa's sickness goes beyond the poison berries to something as strong as hate in Ruby's conjuring; its effects are similar to an attack of the pinks that afflicts Norman Anderson in *Linden Hills.* Even for Willow Springs, uncommon times appear in the wake of the storm. And George, stuck in the middle of confusion, not able to realize *The Tempest* connection, manages to quote from the play itself. When he sees Bernice carrying her dead child to Mama Day at the other place, he declares that "this was the stuff of dreams" (258). As Prospero tells Ferdinand, "We are such stuff / As dreams are made on, and our little life / Is rounded with a sleep" (IV.1.173–75).

Naylor shifts the attention to Cocoa's sickness. For when Abigail comes to the other place to deliver the message to Mama Day that "the Baby Girl is sick" (262), the reader knows that only an issue of life and death could bring Abigail here. Mama Day removes the poison from Cocoa's scalp by cutting off her hair and applying her special paste to Cocoa's head; this much is treatable. However, in conversation with Abigail, Mama Day asks the pivotal question, "How strong is hate?" Abigail's response gives the only combatant she knows: "I believe there's a power greater than hate" (267). It is George's love that can make the difference. He is all the old women have.

But first Mama Day has to visit Ruby. Her placement of

the "circle of silvery powder" (270) around Ruby's home is no secret; Ruby, hiding in the house, knows what is happening as Mama Day calls three times for her to come out. The next event is of Mama Day's doing as well, but the delivery of the storm is more subtle. After leaving the powder, Mama Day warns the workers on the bridge to move away from the water because a storm is coming. And when it does come, the lightning hits the bridge, taking out the day's work, and then hits "Ruby's twice, and the second time the house explodes" (273). Normal storm activity does not include lightning striking the same place twice, but this is Willow Springs with Mama Day simply keeping her word, only after Ruby had made the mistake: "But before I'd let you mess with mine, I'd wrap you up in tissue paper and send you straight to hell" (173). Ruby must be on her way, for after that explosion she and her name are past tense in the novel.[15]

As much as she detested the need to do so, Mama Day sought Dr. Buzzard's help in getting George to the other place. Even though Abigail's words temporarily appear to make the difference—"Please, George, go to the other place" (289)—Dr. Buzzard, in his last words in the novel, says what George most needs to hear—"can you, at least, believe that you ain't the only one who'd give their life to help [Cocoa]" (292). With this proclamation, Buzzard expresses wisdom at the end, much like *The Tempest*'s Caliban whose last words in the play predict a brighter future: "I'll be wise hereafter / And seek for grace" (V.1.351–52). During her days of wait, Mama Day repairs a leak in the roof and while crawling around the attic, she discovers an old ledger that she knows—not through his telling her, but the way that Mama Day knows things—her daddy, John-Paul, had hidden there. The ledger includes a water-stained and smeared illegible bill of sale, a copy of which appears in the front of the book, for the great, grand Mother of them all, but it takes a dream to give Mama Day that woman's name—Sapphira. Next, Mama Day knows she "must go out and uncover the well where Peace died" (283), and she must face the pain of her family in order, finally, to understand. In looking past the pain, with her eyes closed, she sees. The senses work differently on Willow Springs—messages come without words and understanding comes without vision. Her mother, Ophelia, had wanted to go with peace and with Peace; this is the reason John-Paul had to nail shut the old well. It was his hands that prevented her doing so, yet he lost Ophelia to the sound. Mama Day sees her daddy's hands in her hands and knows that those hands must connect with George's hands to be the "bridge for Baby Girl to walk over" (285). Linking George's hands with "all that believing that had gone before" (285) was her only hope.

When George arrives at the other place, Mama Day tells him exactly what she needs from him and that "it ain't gonna be complete unless [she] can reach out with the other hand and take [his]" (294). George cannot hear her words, for he is busy trying to decipher them as metaphor. When Mama Day gives the assignment—go to the chicken coop, take the ledger and John-Paul's walking stick, and bring back whatever he finds under the old red hen—George calls her a fool and lets the ledger and cane fall back into her lap. By the time he reaches Cocoa, her condition scares him profoundly, and he returns to the other place to retrieve the ledger and the walking stick before going to the chicken coop—finally, to do things Mama Day's way even though it makes no sense to him. When Mama Day looks to the sky to elicit support for George, she cannot speak the name Sapphira, for that knowledge has come to her in a dream and it lives outside of the word. Naylor's description of the breeze at George's back, however, suggests Sapphira's response to Mama Day's request. His brief time in the chicken coop is long enough to make him think about what he is doing and to begin to see that his fight with the chicken is preposterous.

He has nothing to show for his mission but bloody hands. He asks the question—"Could it be that she wanted nothing but my hands?" (300)—and then he answers it—"There was nothing that old woman could do with a pair of empty hands" (301). While George thought all Mama Day had said to him was metaphor, the reader is told that Mama Day speaks plain. Her answer to George's question is a resounding "Yes." George is being called on to act without thinking, to respond literally to the words Mama Day speaks; it is for her to decipher their meaning, to make Willow Springs sense out of the task. George goes from the other place, attached symbolically to the past through Sapphira and John-Paul and Mama Day, to the future, attached symbolically to a red hen within the coop. After all, it had been a chicken's egg that was the key to Bernice's pregnancy, and it is the old frizzled hen that alerts Mama Day to Ruby's first conjure on her trailer on the day of Cocoa and George's arrival. To enter this coop is to connect symbolically with a female world—its power and creativity, as Virginia

Fowler points out.[16] In the end, why George goes to the chicken coop is less important than the fact that he does go and that he returns with those empty hands to Mama Day. But this, George cannot do. Instead, he returns to Cocoa, who is across the road, and reaching out for her in his blinding pain, in what must have been a heart attack, at the moment of death, he felt total peace (302). Following the example of Christ, George has given his life for Cocoa. In George's telling, his "heart burst"—literally in failure from his life-long heart problem, perhaps because he did not take his morning pill, and figuratively from a broken heart. His love for Cocoa was too heavy, and in the end, what Buzzard had tried to warn him about, he could not carry all by himself. He refused the help of those who could have made the difference.

After George had been on Willow Springs for a few days, he suggests to Cocoa that he could stay here forever. He gets his wish, but not as he meant it. And years later when Cocoa has stopped grieving for herself and can describe George to his namesake, her child by a second-best new husband, as "a man who looked just like love" (310), she can begin to grieve for George. Only then does Mama Day finally see in Cocoa "a face that's been given the meaning of peace" (312). This last of the Day women has come to terms with the family secrets and its pain. Cocoa has achieved what her grandmother and her mother could not do: she has attained peace.

# CHAPTER FIVE

# *Bailey's Café*

Gloria Naylor's fourth novel, which completes the quartet that serves as the foundation upon which the rest of her career would be built, was published in 1992 by Harcourt Brace Jovanovich. This last novel to date is first in chronological time—1948 and 1949. Home from the second World War, the man who will become the proprietor of Bailey's Café has a wealth of information about the old Negro baseball leagues and an attitude about Jackie Robinson as the choice to integrate the heretofore all-white National and American major leagues. Never referred to by name in the novel and only once as Maestro by his wife, this would-be archangel Michael character with his commentary on how life used to be in the glory days of the Negro Leagues establishes for the reader a world in which it is clear that things are changing.

Readers of *Mama Day* know that in the early 1980s, when George dragged Cocoa up Riverside Drive to Harlem, he identified a brownstone near the pier at 125th Street as the place where he was born and nearby "a deserted, crumbling restaurant stood near the pier. The side windows had been broken, but across the front in peeling letters [Cocoa] could read, Bailey's Café." And George knew, too, that "the man who owned this place found [George] one morning, lying on a stack of newspapers. He called the shelter and they picked [him] up."[1] The time of this fourth novel is the period shortly before George's birth. The unnamed café proprietor who called the shelter is now the maestro who tells the story of the café and the people who find their way there.

The title also represents a return to Naylor's first two novels where she relies on a specific place name, but unlike Brewster Place and Linden Hills, which exist in or near a large Northeastern city, this Bailey's Café can be anywhere. While Naylor's novels all have a mythic quality about them, in this novel she enters fully the realm of magical realism. Many an early reviewer, however, placed Bailey's Café in New York City, for that is its location in *Mama Day.* Gay Wilentz, in the *Women's Review of Books,* rightfully calls it a blues café, but gives it firm location "down a dead-end street at the tip of New York City," while at the same time sees that Naylor "infuses day-to-day living with an alternate, magical reality."[2] Another understands the location of the café, but finds its unsettled geography a mistake, suggesting that "the café, the pawn shop, and the boarding-house have neither the corny power of commercial fantasy nor the poetry of magical realism," which results in a "flawed and misconceived book."[3] For most reviewers, *Bailey's Café* was hailed as a "virtuoso orchestration of survival, suffering, courage and humor,"[4] the "most interesting since her first novel,"[5] and her "finest novel to date."[6] Thomas Jackson, writing for *America,* suggests that she joins "a line of writers as diverse as Sherwood Anderson, Herman Melville and James Baldwin," whom this reviewer sees as those who have contributed to an understanding of America, for "this book, full of pain and sadness yet laced with persistence and love, is ultimately a book about America."[7]

As in her earlier novels, Naylor uses seven as a recurring

number; once again, as in *The Women of Brewster Place,* she has seven stories to tell about the women who come to the café, each one representing a note on a chromatic scale. With a variation on a theme or an improvisation within a set, one of the women is really a man who chooses women's dresses as his outfit of choice and assumes a woman's title. While these women represent the novel's most predominant theme—how a woman's sexuality is shaped by her environment and her heritage—there are more stories to be told beyond the seven. This novel uses musical references to the big band era, to jazz, and specifically to the blues on the various division pages; moreover, it also uses character names as allusions to biblical characters and/or songs. Further, Naylor conceived her story simultaneously as novel and play, and as a play, it had a successful run at the Hartford Stage in Connecticut in April 1994. According to one reviewer, Naylor "sought to present a dramatic equivalent of the great American musical form, the blues, and to explore, through the way her characters speak, the healing value of their finding the rhythms in the pain of their lives."[8]

As a means of understanding the female characters that make their way to Bailey's Café, Ralph Ellison's definition of the blues serves as a guideline: "The blues is an impulse to keep the painful details and episodes of a brutal experience alive in one's aching consciousness, to finger its jagged grain, and to transcend it, not by the consolation of philosophy but by squeezing from it a near-tragic, near-comic lyricism. As a form, the blues is an autobiographical chronicle of personal catastrophe expressed lyrically."[9] Naylor exposes the painful details in each "aching consciousness" within the division of the book entitled "The Jam." In jazz, a jam is a musical session in which various musicians improvise for personal pleasure, but some jam sessions are "institutionalized in concerts."[10] As Naylor records each of the women's stories, she in effect institutionalizes it.

In her earlier novels, Naylor creates a birth experience for Brewster Place, Linden Hills, and Willow Springs. Because Bailey's Café is not similarly locked into specific geography, but "sits right on the margin between the edge of the world and infinite possibility,"[11] the café comes into the world through an integration of a progression of musical terminology and the narrator's own story. Naylor begins the novel with a lullaby for her epigraph. She invokes the blues in this cradle song and announces the birth of "a place never / closing: / Bailey's / Café." The first division page switches the reader's attention to the narrator, who commands the stage: "Maestro, If You Please. . . ." Naylor moves to the language of music when she has the maestro speak to the reader about "a whole set to be played here" for those who want to listen to the music as he stands center stage and sets the tempo (4).

After the tempo has been established through tidbits (4) about himself, the succeeding dividing page is entitled "The Vamp." In musical parlance, a vamp is a simple introductory phrase that can be repeated indefinitely until a soloist enters—those characters that will step forward, one at a time, during the "The Jam." The vamp includes an explanation of the café's menu, and an introduction of Sister Carrie and Sugar Man. These characters sustain the tempo and serve to give credence to the musical phrase "vamp until ready."[12] The reader is reminded that this is the maestro's call, and he will decide when he is ready. After "The Jam," the novel closes with "The Wrap," a term that indicates the music is over; the story has been told. The reader has a new rendering of George's birth, which has the force of sending the reader once more to *Mama Day* to apply this understanding to what George will grow up to tell Cocoa: "I don't have all the pieces. But there are enough of them to lead me to believe that she was not a bitch."[13] The wrap in *Bailey's Café* suggests the sagacity of George's instincts about the mother he never knew.

## "Maestro, If You Please . . ."

The tidbits the maestro discloses about his early years portray a slice of Brooklyn life during the first decades of the twentieth century. His parents were servants to wealthy colored people; as a child, he thought his family must be the only poor colored family. This belief turned out to be instructive because he learned that his perspective on the world was narrow and that he could not draw assumptions about the economic status of all colored people based on the wealthy colored guests that attended his parents' employer's parties. Because his father and his mother had different opinions on every issue, he learned that information on the surface was just that. And what appears to be Naylor's digression into many details about the old Negro baseball leagues is really a purposeful reminder that behind every player, inside every team, there is a story that might not have gotten its due. Later he would use the lessons from these formative years to serve him well at Bailey's Café because "anything really worth hearing in this greasy spoon happens under the surface" (35).

When the maestro mentions that his father had been a bat boy for the Cuban Giants and would have gone barnstorming with the team had he not met his future wife (8), he mentions only the surface tags. The Cuban Giants were the first known black professional team, whose players were "as Cuban as chitlins," for "they were former waiters and porters at the Argyle Hotel in Babylon, Long Island, . . . founded . . . as a summertime divertissement for white vacationers."[14] Barnstorming was not for the weak spirited, for transportation could be by hay wagon, rail car, or rickety bus. Games were played almost every day from early spring to late fall, and in winter, teams went to Florida or California, Cuba or Mexico because "Negro baseball was played the year-round" and "the black baseball player was nearly always a traveling man."[15] The Philadelphia Giants (8) were the team that "breathed life back into eastern blackball,"[16] and Smokey Joe Williams, dubbed the "greatest black pitcher, more remarkable even than the remarkable Satchel Paige" did not leave the Texas League until he was thirty-four. Throwing forty-one victories in 1914, "fanning twenty players" (9) repetitively from 1912 to 1923, and until his retirement in 1932, well past 50 years old, Williams had a fastball that consistently matched Satchel Paige's.[17] The maestro calls him aging in 1917 (9)—though he will play another seventeen years. Even though Naylor includes one of Williams' magical moments in baseball history, the story sheds only a speck of light on his impressive career.

The list which maestro enumerates—the Homestead Grays (Pa.), the Pittsburgh Crawfords, the Baltimore Black Sox, the Chicago American Giants, the Newark Eagles, and the Kansas City Monarchs—are today teams lost in the minutiae of black baseball history. Maestro is convinced that the better ball was being played in the Negro Leagues, but he argues that the League should have opened up to include some good white players—for example, Honus Wagner and Ty Cobb. When he claims a reassignment of color to these white heroes, suggesting that Wagner could just as easily have been called the White Pop Lloyd (10), instead of Lloyd being the Black Honus Wagner, Naylor reminds the reader that the retelling of a history depends on the perspective of the historian. A white sportswriter, when asked in 1938 who was the best player in baseball history, replied, "If you mean in organized baseball, my answer would be Babe Ruth; but if you mean in all baseball . . . the answer would have to be a colored man named John Henry Lloyd,"[18] a shortstop who consistently hit .400 plus a year and was a candidate for any all-time Negro team. Ty Cobb should be the white Oscar Charleston, the maestro suggests, and baseball historians claim that any all-time Negro team would start with Charleston, the best outfielder in the game, who once he gained weight and moved to first base garnered comparisons with Babe Ruth. While a white Josh Gibson "still goes unclaimed" (11) in the mind of the maestro, Gibson's name is most likely to be matched with Babe Ruth. Gibson was called the greatest hitter in Negro baseball, and after Satchel Paige, the most famous among black players.

When the maestro goes off to fight in the second World

War, the public's treatment of his baseball heroes has prepared him for the way in which the public will also treat the black men serving with him, and he uses baseball allusions to make sense of his new environment: "Dorie Miller was the Satchel Paige of the war in the Pacific" (20). Contrary to the maestro's information, Miller (1919–1943) served on the battleship *West Virginia;* the *Arizona* was anchored nearby. The story that exists under the surface is worth repeating, for though Miller shot down the Japanese planes which were dropping torpedoes, he did so having never before shot an antiaircraft machine gun. African Americans were not trained to do so in the early 1940s.[19]

After Pearl Harbor, the maestro was "called up to ship out from Camp Smalls" (20). Naylor's choice of name for the point of embarkation is significant because no such place exists in the *Directory of U.S. Military Bases Worldwide.* However, the name is the same as that of Robert Smalls (1839–1915), a slave who was pressed into duty for the Rebels during the Civil War. Through careful planning, he contrived a plan to slip the Confederate ship, the *Planter,* out of Charleston Harbor before daybreak with fifteen other slaves on board. He then surrendered the ship to the Union forces and became a free man, along with his fellow travelers. During Reconstruction, Smalls served the state of South Carolina, where he had once been a slave, as its congressman.[20] By commemorating this name with a military camp, Naylor calls attention to yet another wartime hero who was underrecognized by his country. And behind that name is a story worth hearing.

Naylor takes six pages to move the maestro through three years in the war. The war takes maestro to the islands of the

South Pacific, but his shifting attitude towards his own efforts in the war can be traced by isolating the dozen times Naylor makes reference to Tokyo. First, a refrain appears five times and always in italics: *"We weren't getting into Tokyo"* (21, 22, 23). The plural pronoun suggests an urgency on the maestro's part to arrive, for if the war were going to be won, it had to be won "on land—the enemy's land" (23). Before he left for war, the maestro had told Nadine that "this would be the most exciting thing to ever happen in [his] life" (21), and the refrain reminds the reader that the maestro wants to see and feel that excitement. Along the way, however, reality sets in—both the underbelly of war with its ceaseless killing, the repetitive soul-numbing combination of activity, weather, and weariness and, for the maestro, his startling awareness of beauty: *"But when the sun rises at the end of the world, the sky and the sea are so blue they only deepen to swallow those streaks of red-gold"* (23). The refrain ceases once the maestro sees, really sees, the beauty, and Tokyo is referred to differently: *"But I couldn't march into Tokyo"* (23). The hawkish maestro becomes a dove, for the horror of getting to Tokyo entwines with his acute awareness of the ocean's color: *"The very young, the deformed, and the old were waiting for me in Tokyo. And you gotta understand how blue it was. How beautiful, soul-wrenching blue"* (25). When the war ends with the atomic bomb, the maestro realizes its simultaneous role in salvation and desecration: "I still believe this country had even been worth Hiroshima happening, but at the very moment of Hiroshima happening, it all stopped being worth it" (27). Both the reader and the maestro learn that this story has a paradoxical interpretation.

Nadine is the maestro's wife, and her presence in his life is one more lesson for the maestro, and one more ploy that Naylor uses to make her point about how to read a person's story. Nadine laughs without making a sound and only speaks when she has something substantial to say. She gives the maestro "a whole different way of looking at . . . women" (19) and becomes his mainstay in his path to understanding that "what happens in life is below the surface." With Nadine, he came to see that "you figure her out or leave her alone" (19); she was not going to help him. His need to know took a back seat to her need to keep it to herself. However, when the maestro returns from the war and finds himself in San Francisco, he is war- and world-weary, and knows only that "life was going to be very different" (27), and it is Nadine who saved him, for she "reached through the fog and touched [his] shoulder" (27).

The flashback tidbits that maestro sets the tempo with (4) end here. What comprises his early years—the childhood and love of baseball, "went to kindergarten" (3), finding and marrying Nadine, "finished up grade school" (3), the war experience, "took [his] first diploma" (3)—work on multiple levels. Each facet is both the thing itself and something else—two ways to read the same story, a story that contradicts and expands. But in the narrative structure, nothing is outside the realm of logical portrayal. In short, even though the recitation is multi-layered, it all makes sense. But when the fog clears for the maestro, and he turns around, Nadine is standing behind him and behind her is "this café" (27). The story continues with the reader in the fog because making logical sense is no longer the narrator's priority; Naylor chooses magical realism, a kind of telling in which imaginary events or images are rendered in a sharply detailed, realistic manner. The maestro finds himself in business in a place called Bailey's Café, and feels no need to tell his customers his real name or his real business. Nadine is his co-conspirator, for she cannot serve the customers lest they "begin thinking [the maestro and Nadine are] actually in the business of running a café" (28). Like the former Bailey, whoever he (or she) might have been—"if there was a Bailey" (28)—the maestro knows the café has to be mobile. Because of his own experience after the war, he knows that there has to be "some space, some place, to take a breather for a while" (28). The maestro and his wife do not run a café at all, but rather a way station—a place to rest. Bailey's Café—like everything the reader has been prepared for by the maestro's tidbits—is more than what it appears to be. It is not for fools. In order to come to Bailey's, the customers have to know what it is and they have to know they need it. The customers already understand depth; there is more to Bailey's than what lies on the surface.

## "The Vamp"

As a musical term, the vamp is a simple introductory phrase that can be repeated indefinitely. During the vamp, the maestro introduces two characters, but they take a back seat to what is repeated indefinitely. The maestro's focus, his band, is Bailey's Café, and the vamp helps the reader gain clarity about how Bailey's Café works. The maestro keeps repeating it, although having to do so annoys him: "New customers are a pain in the butt until they get into the rhythm of things" (31). With one predetermined, never-changing food choice for each weekday and anything a customer wants on the weekend, Bailey's Café takes some getting used to. So the nonexistent menu that the maestro refuses to print becomes a vamp, and he simply repeats the offerings as many times as are necessary.

The two characters that the maestro introduces are Sister Carrie and Sugar Man—two characters that appear to be polar opposites. The first is a cornerstone of the Temple of Perpetual Redemption, one who sees sin waiting to happen all around her, as she judges the world from her self-righteous pedestal; the latter, a pimp in a purple suit, one who sees a way to make a living off the backs of women on their backs. The choice of these two characters is ideal for the maestro's music, for he sees both of them as "one-note players. Flat and predictable" but when taken to a lower key, the maestro can demonstrate that "every point's got a counterpoint" (33–34).

These players, when the lower key sounds, are not the opposites that a first meeting would suggest. First, both Sister Carrie and Sugar Man come to the café only on weekdays. The wide-open choices on the weekend do not provide the comfortable restrictions that these two need. Sister Carrie is "a woman afraid of her own appetites" (33); Sugar Man is content to pay triple the price for the predetermined food that he orders as though it were his choice (33). Further, as the two expose their stories, Sister Carrie worries that her daughter Angel will smell "like a bitch in heat," a projection of her own evil thinking, which causes her to be hypersensitive to the pimping of the

Sugar Man types of the world. On the other hand, Sugar Man sees himself as a protector, a refuge for angels who need "a shoulder to lean on when they have to cry" (34). For girls who were going to travel this path anyway, he can be their pillar of support. In the lower key, Sister Carrie's giving way to her carnal desires would depend on Sugar Man's providing the necessary strength that women need in this world. To Sugar Man, Sister Carrie is a dried stick, and to her, he is filth and scum (33), but that is on the surface, and anything "really worth hearing . . . happens under the surface" (35).

## "The Jam"

The Maestro has prepared the reader for the performances of the seven major players who solo during the jam. Like the seven women on Brewster Place in her first novel, Naylor delivers another community of women, whose lives are sustained and enhanced by the company they keep. The pain they have endured is made bearable because they have found the way station and the people who can become the props they have never had. *Brewster Place* has Eva Turner, the woman who knows that Mattie Michael, upon first seeing her, is in trouble and needs help; *Bailey's Café* has Eve, who runs the boarding house, "right down the block from this café" (80); she is the maestro's first customer. But before the reader can hear Eve's story and explore the community of women, Naylor, in the longest story, begins with a woman who separates herself from the community, whose pathetic situation is made even more so by her own isolation from the community of women and from a man who offers her love too late to make a difference.

## "Mood: Indigo"

Naylor chooses to insert a colon between the two words of the chapter title she selects for Sadie's story, but the reference is to Duke Ellington's 1931 highly popular "Mood Indigo." The lyrics lament that it is not possible to really know the blues until the singer claims "that feelin' goes stealin' down to my shoes," which is the result of "my baby [saying] goodbye." The words of the song have a literal interpretation in Sadie's case; for in her life these words are no exaggeration: "I'm so lonesome I could cry; Cause there's nobody who cares about me; I'm just a soul who's bluer than blue can be. When I get that mood indigo, I could lay me down and die."[21]

The setting of Sadie's early days is Chicago's South Side, an area that grew with the massive southern migration of African Americans from the South. Naylor's geography in this novel follows the development of jazz, for New Orleans jazz finds its home in Chicago's South Side where in the 1920s cabarets and dance halls flourished. Sadie was the inadvertent result of a failed abortion, called by her mother "The One The Coat Hanger Missed" so many times that she believed that it was her name (41). As she grows older, Sadie's mother screams her name when she beats her, primarily because she had not been aborted.

Sadie is another form of the name Sarah and is reminiscent

of the biblical Sarah in several unexpected ways. First, Sarah is
barren during all her childbearing years; Sadie is barren
because her mother has her sterilized at fourteen, doing it for
her because her "life woulda been pure hell ever having to take
care of a child" (45). Second, on two accounts in Genesis, one
before the name change, Abram introduces Sarai as his sister,
in an effort to save his own life. In a time of famine in Canaan,
and because she is a woman "beautiful to behold," Abram fears
she will be taken, and he will be killed. As his sister and not his
wife, he is allowed to live, but she is taken into Pharaoh's
house as part of his harem (Genesis 12:10–20). However, the
Lord intervenes on her behalf and sends afflictions on Pharaoh,
who takes Abram to task before sending him and his wife on
their way. Later, in Genesis 20, after their names change, Abraham once again introduces Sarah as his sister—this time to
Abimelech, who immediately sends for her and takes her as his
own. Before anything happens, however, God sends a dream to
Abimelech to warn him that Sarah is another man's wife. When
Abraham is asked why he has perpetrated this scheme, he
admits his fear of losing his life in a place where there is no fear
of God, and besides, "she is indeed [his] sister, the daughter of
[his] father but not the daughter of [his] mother, and she
became [his] wife" (Genesis 20:12). On each occasion, Sarah is
not consulted about her feelings; she is simply offered as sister
and then promptly taken by the reigning authority. Any fear
which she may have felt in both situations is simply not
addressed.

Such is the case with Naylor's Sadie. Her mother took her
on the streets when she was just thirteen because she had been

"selling [her] tail all this time to feed [Sadie] till [she was] sick and near death" (44). It was time for Sadie to "kick in too" (44). As in the Bible, here also was a case of mistaken identity. Though her mother said Sadie was but thirteen, no man believed it. The first one liked it when she screamed until he discovered that the "wetness covering his groin and stomach wasn't sweat" (45). Like Abraham, Sadie's mother, was chastised: *"What kind of woman are you?"* (45), but in Sadie's world there is no benevolent God who stops the unwelcome advance. The second account specifies the incident with the abortionist. When Sadie finds herself pregnant within six months, her mother finds a lowlife willing to "earn the extra fee." So in a filthy room, "smelling of dogs and cats," he goes inside Sadie a second time with a scalpel to make certain her mother will not be inconvenienced ever again (45). Like her biblical namesake, Sadie is never asked her feelings, and her fear is not addressed.

Sadie learns early that her "only way out of [the intolerable home situation] was to love" (42), and in an ironic inversion of First Corinthians, Naylor uses a key verse to plot the disintegration of and challenge to Sadie's mission. The verse declares "so faith, hope, love abide, these three; but the greatest of these is love" (I Corinthians 13:13). Faith leaves with her "daddy on an errand for a pint of milk"; Hope joins him when he never returns from the trip; Charity (or love) is her good fortune at her father's not "cutting the squalling throat of his newborn bastard" (42). For Sadie, love is the greatest of these three because love alone has not deserted her. That she has life is her understanding of love's meaning. In the end, she will be the one to walk out on love, and, therefore, life. Sadie's desire to be good emanates from a deep-seated need for her own survival in a world where her mother is killing herself with a quart-a-day addiction to absinthe, which was "rotting her brain" (42). Absinthe is sixty-eight percent alcohol, made of wormwood and other herbs, and now banned in most Western countries.

Sadie's early years, though it is an injustice to refer to them as any kind of childhood, are separated by the time before and after her life on the streets. Before and after, her dreams always end the same way; the goal is to please her mother, to hear her mother say, "I'm proud of you. You're a good girl, Sadie" (44, 46). In the innocence of the former years, Sadie dreams of finding success as a secretary, teacher, or nurse. Everything about this world is clean—the work she does, the home she creates with a garden of red roses. After her indoctrination to the ugly reality into which she is pushed, however, the dreams of success are a hyperbolic extension of her daily routine—multiple partners one after the other with no rest in between, group, anal, and oral sexual activity with old, ugly, and deformed johns. In her dreams, she measures success by taking "it in the behind" and not gagging when she takes it in the mouth, but making her tricks believe she likes it (46). In this sordid world, the money she makes buys a clean place to live. Decency of work is sacrificed for the dream of a clean home. But Sadie's dreams are just that, and when her mother succumbs to absinthe poisoning, all Sadie hears in the end is the lifelong repetitive curse: "Look at what I come to, trying to feed you. Just look at what I come to" (46).

Naylor gives Sadie only dreams to sustain her. Three years

in the upscale whorehouse provide a release from life on the streets, but deny her any possibility of positive growth. Sadie uses her dreams to focus on a man thirty years her senior who delivers wood to the whorehouse, who speaks her name when she tells him without looking at him. For three years she lives for the "sound of her name in his mouth" (49). When the whorehouse closes and she meets him for what she believes to be a final time, hoping only to find out his name, which he has not bothered to say in three years, the brief conversation of five minutes, resulting in a marriage proposal, becomes the longest one they will have in the next quarter century of life together. In Naylor's ironic choice of Daniel for the name, the silent, quiet-drinking man, has a biblical namesake whose gift is dream interpretation. Sadie lives out the middle years of her life trying to defy the odds of converting the dirty shack by the railroad tracks into the white-bungalow-with-green-picket-fence of her dreams. The red roses of her dreams become red geraniums. In flower lore, the scarlet geranium stands for comfort, stupidity, and folly.[22] The geraniums are the single possession that Sadie is willing to fight for with the man who was "the closest thing that she would ever have to what she'd dreamed of" (52). "They leave, I leave" (55), she told Daniel when he smashed the first pot. Those flowers were her comfort; to Daniel, they were her folly.

After Daniel's death and the loss of that home and eventually those flowers, Sadie reverts to the only path in life that can make her dreams live. At this point in the narrative, the maestro re-enters Sadie's story to remind the reader the importance of dreams: "My father used to tell me that a star dies in heaven every time you snatch away someone's dream" (64). The unidentified footsteps that come "slowly from the far edge of the settlement" (65), who bring her the first comfort after she has realized that all is lost, are a kind of Christian soldier, a symbol of dreamkeeping. They are tending to the least, as Matthew records Jesus having said, and the food she reaches into the crumbled bag for resonates with Christian symbolism—"the gift of bread and fish" (65). But for Sadie to keep those dreams, she needs the cheap sweet wine with five stars on the label. Through the hallucinations that the wine creates for her once she downs a flat pint bottle, the world becomes what she has always dreamed it to be—rainbows streak the roof, greens fill the yard, and bright red spots speckle the dead geranium leaves (65). The star-studded wine becomes the only way she can see stars in this world. In pursuit of the wine, she becomes a two-bit whore; from the streets of Chicago, she finds her way into Bailey's café.

Once Sadie arrives at the café, Naylor's language moves toward magical realism, making the café "the last place before the end of the world" (68). Sadie's welcome is determined by Nadine, who serves her on the house because Sadie is capable of turning the "thick mugs into fine bone china" (68) by the way she reaches out to receive her tea. With Sadie paying visits to the café, the narrative structure returns to the 1948 present. Sister Carrie from the vamp returns to repeat her biblical views, this time in front of another nemesis, Eve, whose solo in the jam appears after Sadie's has concluded, and Iceman Jones, the man who will offer Sadie the love she has never experienced. When the iceman sees Sadie's eyes, the same eyes that had scared Daniel and caused him to avoid looking into them for twenty-five years, he knows immediately that they are "the eyes of a four-year-old dreaming to survive" (70). Because the iceman has spent a lifetime looking in "so many iceboxes, which tells a whole story about somebody's life, he's also learned that most things aren't what they seem" (70). Jones knows the maestro's vamp—"anything really worth hearing . . . happens under the surface" (35). As the two begin a relationship, Jones finds in Sadie someone to care about, someone who listens to his day; in him, she finds someone with whom she can live her dreams in her mind.

Significantly, Iceman introduces himself to Sadie; how rare this simple occurrence is in her life is indicated by the manner in which she tells her name, "turn[ing] her head to the side as if expecting a blow" (71). In her mind, represented by italics in the novel, she invites Iceman to the picket fence she never did have in life. Later, in her mind, he visits her front porch where for the first time in her life she imagines what it must be like to share a joke: "*But there was laughter on her front porch. For the first time, there was laughter*" (74). When Sadie, in her mind, experiences laughter, Naylor alludes to the biblical Sarah's response when God tells Abraham she will bear a son—Sarah laughed (Genesis 18:12). And finally, in her mind, she extends an invitation to dinner, plans the meal, and uses her best Waterford crystal. He comes, in her mind, and they share the meal, discovering that it is "*easy to feel at home with this man. And she would keep him in her home, since it seemed he wanted to stay*" (77).

Sadie is capable of playing out the developing relationship with the iceman in her mind because in reality he is present in her life, giving her her first real kiss (76), offering to share with her what he has: "What I have, you'll have. What I eat, you'll eat. Wherever I lay my head, there's a place for you" (77). The iceman's proposal to Sadie echoes George's promise to Cocoa in *Mama Day,* the promise he repeats on the phone to Mama Day before they meet and she, in turn, explains to Abigail: "If he got a nickel, she's got a part in it. He got a dream, he's gonna take her along. If he got a life, Abigail, he's saying that life can open itself up for her."[23] The same language Naylor uses for the iceman is also repeated in the words of Ruth Scott, a woman Naylor interviewed in Robinsonville, Mississippi, about her life-long friend, Hester Hall: "She can stay here with me long as she want to. If I eat, she gonna eat; if I sleep, she gonna sleep. If I ain't got nothing but a cotton house, she got a corner."[24] In her mind, Sadie already has Iceman Jones, so in reality, she refuses him; he offers the moon, but even that, at this point for Sadie, cannot replace her alcoholic dependence on the stars (78).

Naylor's placement of Iceman Jones's proposal comes after he has asked her to dance. Because of Sadie's addiction, Naylor directs them out the café's back door, into "nothing. . . . Since the place sits right on the margin between the edge of the world and infinite possibility, the back door opens out to a void" (76). That dance out the back is Naylor's way of helping the maestro explain to the reader that it is the end of the line for Sadie. Had they danced out the front door, infinite possibility would have awaited.

## "Eve's Song"

Proprietor of her boardinghouse/bordello, Eve has been in the neighborhood for twenty-five years when the maestro and Nadine take ownership of Bailey's Café. She arrived in New Orleans in 1913, stayed ten years, and then left, eventually to open her boardinghouse and plant her garden. In 1948, she becomes the café's first customer and one of the topics the maestro wants to discuss. First on his list is a reference to "the Indians closing in on the pennant," with the help of "Larry Doby from the Negro Leagues along with the immortal pitching arm of Satchel Paige" (79). The Indians won the American League pennant that year and went on to beat the Boston Braves of the National League in the World Series, 4–2. Larry Doby had the highest batting average for the Indians in the Series, .318, while Paige saw little action.[25] His reference to the first-time availability of an automatic transmission on 1948 Chevrolets is clear enough, and the last item of discussion, besides Eve, was the Truman-Dewey Presidential race. The maestro did not like the incumbent Democrat Truman because he had permitted the bomb to drop on Japan, not once but twice. His opponent, Thomas E. Dewey, Republican Governor of New York, had much popular support, most likely because he was known to the public as a "racket-busting district attorney and as a progressive governor who managed to cut taxes in his first term and still maintain a $623 million surplus."[26] When the maestro says he will vote for Truman because he prefers one he does not like to one he does not trust, he believes, according to the papers that were predicting a victory for Dewey, that he is in the minority. In fact, in the fall Dewey goes down in defeat. These historical moments—Truman's victory and the Indians' title—contribute to the background celebratory mood at the end of the novel.

Eve's boardinghouse, out the café's front door and to the right, operates in much the same way that the café does: you can only find it if you need it. The women who find Eve do so because they need a place to stay, and have been successful at seeing the garden, which can be seen only by those whose need and awareness are ripe (81). The characters from the vamp reappear in Eve's chapter; this time, they are unnamed and unidentified, but the reader knows them from their lines as they sound the same repetitive note. Sister Carrie's voice condemns: "They're all sluts and whores and tramps" (80), while Sugar Man's voice echoes his counterpoint: "She's got a good game going, and the nerve to bad-mouth me. Every pimp don't need to wear pants" (80). Their appearance prepares the reader for Eve's solo, a reminder to listen under the surface. Unlike Sadie, Eve speaks in first person; she, not the maestro, tells her own story.

Eve's name is an obvious reference to the first woman, created by God out of Adam's rib. Naylor's Eve is created by her Godfather, who claims "he found [her] in a patch of ragweed, so new [she] was still tied to the birth sac" (83). Like the biblical Eve, she has no earthly mother or father; unlike her namesake, though, she has no Adam. Naylor explores what can happen when no male partner is present. The biblical Eve's role in Genesis moves from giving Adam the apple, being cast out from the Garden of Eden, to "being known" by Adam and conceiving a son, then repeating for a second son. All of her activity and existence is involved with Adam's. She does not significantly function alone in the world. Without that male partner, Naylor's Eve faces problems that begin with the development of her breasts. Both men and women of the town begin to read their own stories of and about her sexuality. Men were simple to read as they "had only one question in their eyes," which she instinctively knew how to answer: "[Godfather] would kill us both with his bare hands" (83). The women are more complicated, more unnatural in what their eyes asked. The more these women's eyes asked, the more Eve realized that she "was now forced to go through months and months with no one and nothing to touch [her]" (83). It was the "righteous righteous" women (85) upon whom Eve would place the greatest blame.

The setting for Eve's early days is the Plaquemines peninsula, southeast of New Orleans, east of the delta, as the biblical Garden of Eden is in the east (Genesis 2:8). The towns that Eve must plod through when she is cast out of Pilottown on her way to Arabi appear on the state map of Louisiana. Arabi is located just outside of New Orleans, the first home of jazz in the United States. The activity that incites her Godfather and causes her dismissal is the "stomp, Billy, stomp" game, which he views as a sinful machination of self-pleasure. Eve casts herself upon her mother earth because she has been denied any kind of touch, and in the process realizes that the vibrations caused by Billy's stomping make her feel good all over. The reference to the "stomp, stomp" also plays on the beat of the music that mixes ragtime and swing, a style that was becoming popular around New Orleans at the time of Eve's arrival in the city.

When Eve left Pilottown, she was naked, just as she was when her Godfather brought her into his world. She took that naked self and covered and packed it with mud, so that when she arrived in New Orleans, she was "neither male nor female" (91), only mud. The biblical first man was created out of "dust from the ground" that had been watered from mist (Genesis 2:6–7), so Naylor's use of mud suggests that Eve gave birth anew to herself. Her story suggests that her life in New Orleans was a preparation for the business she would later expand in a new location, one where women could find her when they needed her. In New Orleans, she had made a good deal of dollars, "not one of them earned on [her] back; and a love of well-kept gardens" (91). A reminder of the Garden of Eden from which her biblical namesake had been dismissed, Naylor's Eve manages a return to the Garden where she grows flowers year round, no matter the weather. Each of the women that contribute to the jam has a favorite flower, and Eve's is the lily, all varieties. According to flower lore, the lily stands for majesty, "demanding the company and contrast of other flowers to make its majestic impression"; it is also an emblem of virgin purity.[27] All of Eve's other flowers are for sale; only the lily cannot be bought. Its place in the center of her garden, standing alone in all its varieties, anchors those other flowers—the same role that Eve plays in her boardinghouse for the women who have come because they need to be able to depend on her.

## "Sweet Esther"

The maestro, who has seen Esther only one time, instantly reads the look in her eyes. Though it is summer, her presence in a corner of the room "turned [it] into a block of ice"; the maestro read that kind of power as hate (94). She speaks only one word, "Eve," and it would be to Eve alone that she would tell her story. In Esther's solo during the jam, she tells her own story, but because parts of her life are unspeakable, the reader has to go under the surface to understand the source of the hate that the maestro reports.

The title of her solo—"Sweet Esther"—plays on the myriad number of songs that begin with "Sweet" followed by a female name—Adeline, Alice, Caroline, Ellie Rhee, Eloise, Genevieve, Georgia Brown, Jane, Kate, Kitty Clover, Lorraine, Marie, Nelly, Polly Oliver, Rosie O'Grady, and Betsy from Pike, to name a few. In praise of a woman's best virtues, the songwriter's narrator is usually the adoring lover/admirer. Because Naylor's Esther plays her own song, she tells her story with all the self-effacing honesty that Eve detects in her face; this honesty is her best virtue.

Her biblical namesake is one of only two women whose names—Esther and Ruth—title a book in the Bible. The biblical Esther is raised by her cousin, Mordecai, who adopts her as his daughter after her parents die. Word goes out that King

Ahasuerus is replacing his Queen Vashti because she refused to come to him when he called her through his eunuchs. The beautiful young virgin who pleased him most would take her place and become the new queen. Esther joined the other young virgins who were placed in the care of Hegai, with whom they would spend twelve months in a period of beautifying themselves. When it was Esther's turn to step from the harem, she took the advice of Hegai and pleased Ahasuerus the most and became his queen. Naylor's Esther is also raised by a relative, her brother, who is kind to her, like Mordecai was to his Esther. Her brother calls her only little sister (95), the only name she will respond to when she takes residence in Eve's basement. When she is twelve years old, her brother "marries" her to his employer, again as Mordecai does his Esther. She is visited and prepared for the day by a hag, a woman who has characteristics of a man, such as long gray hairs on her chin (96). The biblical Hegai is a eunuch, a man who has been castrated so that he may be trusted in his work with the King's harem, who takes on some characteristics of a woman. The two striking differences in the two women is that the biblical Esther is beautiful and Naylor's Esther is not; the biblical Esther is treated with respect, listened to by the king, and becomes the savior of the Jews, while Naylor's Esther, still a child, becomes the victim of sexual abuse in the hands of a man who forces her into sado-masochistic activity.

In the home of the "husband," the hag that waits upon Esther gives her a daily treatment with cream that "costs more to buy than [her] brother's miserable shack" (96). A vague connection exists between that cream application and the events that occur in the cellar. The unnamed man's question to the hag is "when will [she] be ready," and hearing "soon" is enough for him to begin "to call [her] into the cellar" (97). The spacious fairy princess bedroom she has been given is hers alone; it is only in the cellar where Esther begins to understand that "in the dark, words have a different meaning" (97). Five times in italics the refrain is given: "*We won't speak about this, Esther*" (95, 96, 97, 98, 99). These words come into the story line at every occasion when Esther is about to verbalize the horrors she has lived with and through, but that echoing voice in her own head stops her, redirects her, silences the descriptive words she could say. The reader knows that she kneels in the cellar and over time learns the use of "leather-and-metal things" (97).

She is isolated from the world, and she is from an unidentified place, the only boarder at Eve's whose specific home has been too unbearable to name. In that place, wherever it was, she had no friends, no means to learn, except through the radio with its songs of kissing and love-making, the nature of which she can only wonder. The radio also provides her with "The Shadow," a favorite show which becomes her company in the dark and words to call what happens there—they "make evil" (98). "The Shadow" was a highly popular radio mystery series that lasted from 1930–1954. Each episode began with the line, "Who knows what evil lurks in the hearts of men? The Shadow knows!" followed by a heinous laugh. The detective, a Lamont Cranston, had learned how to make himself invisible, and he used this knowledge to be successful in bringing evil-doers to justice.[28] Esther's hope that the Shadow would appear in her cellar, invisible, and bring this evil to an end sustained her until she realized that perhaps the Shadow was there because "he enjoys to stand there and watch" (98). Even her own fantasies let her down.

When Esther takes up residence in the basement of Eve's boardinghouse, Eve removes the light bulbs so that gentleman callers will not have to look at her eyes, the ones in which the maestro saw pure hate, and the same eyes that Eve claims contribute to shaping "the most honest face of any woman [she] knows" (99). The men that visit her always bring white roses and call her little sister (99). Only in Eve's magical garden are white roses available all year long, for Eve makes sure they are always obtainable for Esther's callers. White roses symbolize silence, and the men who come to Esther mimic the god of silence, who is often "represented as a young man, half-naked, holding a finger to his lips and with a white rose in the other hand."[29] Naylor's linking the white rose with Esther suggests a message to the reader that is a recurring theme in "Sweet Esther": *We won't speak about this, Esther.* In Eve's basement Esther no longer fears the abuse she endured for those twelve years in the monster's home, but the memory of those days are reflected in the hate that remains in her eyes; the white rose is a sign that even at Eve's she cannot speak about that part of her life. The refrain plays on.

## "Mary (Take One)"

Each description of Mary leads the reader towards a deeper understanding of her beauty; it is so powerful that it weighs on her—informing, directing, and dictating every move she makes. Her earliest memories are shaped by her own reflection as seen in the eyes of men who cannot help being dazzled by her beauty. From her father she learns she is beautiful. He gives her the nickname Peaches because of her skin texture and color: "Plump and sweet. Yellow and sweet" (102), the name itself suggesting a succulent morsel, temptingly desirable, ready to be devoured in a single swallow. As she grows up, his over-zealous desire to protect her from other males, those of all ages, gives her a muted message that she understands somewhere outside of language. When would-be suitors come, her father asks, "why?," wanting to hear them admit the reason: "Cause he was really saying, I already know why you want to see my daughter, and you know I know why" (103). As she tries to read her world, the mirrors into which she gazes—the literal ones that hang in her room and the eyes of those into which she looks—send conflicting messages that contribute to her awareness that she must be two people: "a whore and . . . Daddy's baby" (104). The choirmaster, supposedly a trusted church staff member, begins the rip into her nine-year-old psyche when he places his hand "under [her] blouse" (104). As Mary plays out her turn in the jam, the language of her story alternates between first and third person: "In horror I watched her grow up, and I learned to hate her for breaking my father's heart" (105).

This take one on Mary has a biblical counterpart most likely in Mary Magdalene. Though there are seven women in the New Testament with the name Mary, one or more could be the same Mary. Mary Magdalene, however, is the one mentioned first in each listing of the group of females who followed and served Jesus from the beginning of his ministry, "women who had been healed of evil spirits and infirmities: Mary, called Magdalene, from whom seven demons had gone out" (Luke 8: 2). Through a point of view that bears similarities to Naylor's Mary, one scholar tells it this way: "Mary Magdalene's family was one of those great Sadducean families. . . . At the age of thirteen or fourteen, already radiantly beautiful and completely developed, as women are at that young age in [Greece], her mind sharp like the minds of all the daughters of her race, saucy and sensual, she lived surrounded by music and perfumed young snobs . . . , read aloud from the *Symposium* Diotima's speech on free love as the best means of attaining wisdom, or [listened to talk] about Phryne the courtesan," and further, this Mary Magdalene was "beautiful enough to upset the spheres and knowing that she was so, a girl who lived day and night in intimate complicity with seven demons who put fire into her veins."[30] Mary Magdalene met Jesus, had her demons removed, and was converted; Naylor's Mary thought she might find solace in a man who simply asked for her name: "Before we even get started, tell me your real name" (109).

Even though he uses her real name repeatedly, the sound of it could only temporarily seduce her, for the eye-mirrors she meets on trains are too strong a reminder of the demons that remain in her. After she gouges a beer opener into her cheek and rips apart her face, she refuses cosmetic surgery for her scar. The time had come to find her way to Eve's. As Mary tells her story, in the mirror that are Eve's eyes, she sees only the scar reflected back to her, and it is the scar itself that becomes, through Eve, beautiful (112). Though Sugar Man wants to claim her for his stable, Mary has found the rest stop she needs at Eve's.

She makes her way to Eve's from Kansas City, another city where jazz exploded during the 1920s and 1930s. The addresses Naylor gives—Twelfth and Highland. Eighteenth and Vine (106)—are associated with jazz nightclubs that flourished in that neighborhood during those decades: Cherry Blossom, Lone Star, Lucille's Band Box, Reno Club, and Roscoe Hall. At the corner of Eighteenth and Vine was the Subway Club, the specific club in which Naylor has Mary employed, the one in which she meets the small, crippled gambler: "The straight razor was the first thing [she] noticed about him when he came into Piney Brown's" (108). With Brown as its manager, the Subway was known for its all-star jam sessions, attracting musicians who played in the bands of Fletcher Henderson and Count Bassie.[31]

Mary's gentlemen callers purchase daffodils from Eve's garden in order to pay her a visit. Naylor's choice of a flower that belongs to the narcissus family suggests a link between Mary and the most famous narcissus myth, that of Narcissus himself. As Mary is haunted by the woman she sees in mirrors, the youthful Narcissus falls in love with the reflection of himself in a mountain pool of water. So infatuated is he with the beauty of what he sees that he cannot leave the site; he stares endlessly into this reflecting mirror. He dies still looking at his own face and is turned into the narcissus flower. The daffodil, the jonquil, and the narcissus are all kinds of the narcissus, and it is difficult to determine "where one leaves off and the others begin."[32]

When Daddy Jim comes to Bailey's Café in search of his Peaches, the maestro informs him "no one knows her by that name" (100), and even when he is taken by Sugar Man to Eve's, he continues to refer to her as Peaches. Three times, Eve tells him, "I'll return her to you whole" (113, 114). Her name takes on a symbolic significance—Peaches is the whore, the little girl with promise (104); Mary is her Daddy's good girl, the one who has to learn to look in the mirrors of the men's eyes who visit her at Eve's with their bouquets of daffodils, to take her time, to "look in that mirror good, and accept no less than what [she] deserves" (113). Mary's wholeness, in part, is based on her coming to understand that she can define herself, that the mirror that seduced Narcissus, causing his death, does not have to repeat its script in her life. Eve predicts that the daffodil-carriers will decrease in number until there is no one else waiting (114). She makes a promise to Mary's father, one that is different from the promise that her father's friends proclaimed—the ones who held Peaches on their knees and touched the soft curls of her head (104). Even though Eve shuts the door in his face, she calls him friend and makes a promise that does not divide, but heals: "I'll return your daughter to you whole" (114).

## "Jesse Bell"

Unlike the other women who reside at Eve's place, Jesse Bell flagrantly disregards Eve's rules, cowering for no one. Ignoring Eve's after-midnight curfew to play rummy with the maestro in his long, slow early morning hours, she has her own opinions about those among whom she dwells. She reads their surface stories, however, for Esther is little more than one who attracts "every sleazeball pervert within fifty miles" (117) and Mary is reduced to the "nympho next door" (117). She lets the maestro know that she is no Shirley Temple (117). At the time of their conversation, the child actress, born in 1928, was a year away from retirement from the movies at the age of 21. Beginning her career at the age of 4, Shirley Temple was one of the great moneymakers of motion pictures throughout the 1930s and 1940s. Her curls, dimples, and sparkling, innocent personality were known to all; Jesse Bell's reference to the child actress is a measure by which the maestro can understand how distantly removed she is from any naiveté. Jesse Bell has found her way to Eve's because she is a heroin addict who wants to get this "monkey off [her] back" (118). Alone among the others, Jesse Bell is at Eve's by personal invitation from this "icy icy mama" (118) who had extended her card on one of her good will mission moments to Jesse Bell when she was locked away on the lower level in the house of detention. When the reader first meets Jesse Bell, she has undergone a cure for her addiction twice, so Jesse Bell knows that Eve is a female match for her former husband's Uncle Eli, the hardest man she has ever known.

Naylor's choice of the name Eli as Jesse's nemesis suggests a parallel with the antagonism that existed between the biblical Jezebel and Elijah. Jezebel was a Phoenician princess who married King Ahab and encouraged him to worship the false god Baal with her. The prophet Elijah warned the people to abandon Baal, and then proceeded, with the Lord's help, to seize and kill many of the prophets of Baal. When Ahab reported to Jezebel what Elijah had accomplished, she sent him a powerful message: "So may the gods do to me, and more also, if I do not make your life as the life of one of them by this time tomorrow" (1 Kings 19:2). Elijah feared for his life and left town. But her brief victory did not last, for Elijah returned with a curse from the Lord: "The dogs shall eat Jezebel within the bounds of Jezreel" (1 Kings 21:23). This prophecy came to pass, for when Jehu came to Jezreel, he gave the order for Jezebel to be thrown from her window, "so they threw her down; and some of her blood spattered on the wall and on the horses, and they trampled on her" (2 Kings 9:33). When they went to bury her, "they found no more of her than the skull and the feet and the palms of her hands" (2 Kings 9:35). The dogs had eaten her flesh, as Elijah had declared through the words of the Lord.

Naylor's Jesse Bell came from a long line of Bells, tough longshoremen who respected their women and also had to be tough to make it in this world. Like any character who sought a home on Tupelo Drive in *Linden Hills,* Uncle Eli wanted to forget he was black. He wanted to be like "white folks"—not the "honest ofays" but the "dicty" ones (125). Both references to white people, these slang expressions found their way into print by 1928 and 1931, respectively, but were most likely a part of spoken language for many years. An *ofay* is believed to be *foe* in pig Latin, and *dicty* means "stylish, high class, wealthy."[33] Like her biblical counterpart, Jesse Bell also marries a king, one who would give her the biggest brownstone in Sugar Hill (122). Though she had some small moments of victory over Uncle Eli—teaching her husband and other family members how to love the kind of food her mother had raised her on, which Uncle Eli called "slave food" (124), and referring to her husband as Mister Bell when Eli refused to call her Mrs. King (125)—in the end, Uncle Eli won in all the important ways: over time, he took her son and publicly exposed her relationship with her lesbian lover. The biblical Jezebel's being devoured by dog echoes in the metaphors Naylor selects for Jesse Bell: all was reduced to "dog shit" (131). The nineteen good years she had put into her marriage with the man she loved "went straight to the dogs" (118), for Uncle Eli was a murderer and she became just a smell of something decayed (118). Just as the biblical Jezebel "painted her eyes, and adorned her head, and looked out the window" (2 Kings 9:30), Jesse Bell was put "on display like a painted dummy in a window" (131).

In the late 1920s, Jesse Bell had met her King at the Savoy in New York's Harlem. The Savoy opened in the mid 1920s and billed itself as the "World's Most Beautiful Ballroom"; it attracted some of the best jazz bands in the business.[34] On the night she meets her future husband, she is with her unnamed special friend, referred to only this way in her jam because what is particularly important to Jesse is that she let the reader know that her husband knows—and understands—about this woman (123, 125, 128, 130, 131): "when you're into women as much as he was, [she believed that he did] understand that somebody else might feel the same way about 'em at times like you do" (125). But there is a judgment placed on Jesse's search for women because it is from one of them that "someone slipped a little paper envelope of white powder in [her] hand"

(130–31). Though heroin was no stranger to jazz clubs during this time, and even Billie Holiday's addiction was well known, Naylor links the lesbianism and the heroin. As her addiction mounts—the progression from sniffing, to popping, to mainlining—the white horse is all Jesse lives for until she sees that it is also what she might die for.

Sister Carrie, with her vamp, interrupts Jesse's jam. Carrie wants to quote for her from Ezekiel, but Eve's presence in Bailey's Café turns the pointed self-righteous sermon into a duel. All of the verses that Carrie sings out come from Ezekiel 16—as they appear in the text, verses 32, 38, 25 (134), 30, 52 (135), and, in italics, verse 6 (136)—and all have to do literally with committing adultery and its attendant punishment. The fact that Ezekiel 16 is an allegory of the unfaithful Jerusalem is lost on Sister Carrie. Eve reminds her that she should try Isaiah 12, but before she can shout it out, the maestro intervenes. This six-verse chapter contains two short psalms of praise and thanks for the Lord's comfort and salvation. Eve knows what Jesse has gone through to break that addiction, and the language that Jesse uses to explain it to the maestro once again echoes the biblical Jezebel's fall to death: "you're speeding along at . . . seventy miles an hour. And suddenly your whole body slams right into this big brick wall. But you don't go unconscious, so you can feel crushed pieces of your skull stabbing back into your brain, your lungs collapsing in, each bone snapping and crumbling, your insides busting open as your guts rip apart. That's how much it hurts" (138–39). Then, she explains, you do it again the next day. In spite of all this pain, once she is off, Eve gives her a new heroin kit, and Jesse Bell uses up the twelve bags that come with it. Then the cold turkey cure is repeated, followed by yet another, nicer heroin kit. Eve knows that Jesse has to learn to stop blaming someone else for her troubles and assume responsibility for herself. She alone has to be strong enough not to return to heroin.

Jesse Bell's flower is the dandelion, a weed that Eve would under ordinary circumstances eliminate from her garden, but, like all the women she cares for, Jesse's is a special case (117). The dandelion has been called the tramp with the golden crown, but all of the parts of this weed can be used—the leaves, stems, flowers, and roots—for various foods, a high source of vitamin A. For Jesse Bell, "the tramp from the docks" (118), Naylor chooses a weed that symbolizes both grief and bitterness, one that early Flemish and German painters used in pictures of the Crucifixion to suggest the suffering of Christ,[35] in which salvation is included. Jesse Bell has looked out the back door of Bailey's Café and known hell. Because she has fought back twice from that searing free fall she described to the maestro, while teetering on the brink, it is still the front door of infinite possibility (76) through which she enters from and returns to Eve's.

## "Mary (Take Two)"

The maestro, who introduces each of the jams, is not present for this one. Rather, the mostly silent Nadine steps forward to share the stage with Eve. In alternating voices, they present Mariam's story. Mariam speaks only six words in a repeating refrain six times: *"No man has ever touched me"* (143–46).

This is the core of her story. When the tale moves backwards in time to Ethiopia, the narrative voice knows the thoughts, concerns, and actions of Mariam's mother, but in a novel in which magical realism presides over logic, these parts of the story can also be known by Eve, in the mysterious ways that she understands all of the women who come to her. While each of them is a special case, this second Mary breaks all the rules in the "relay for broken dreams" (144). The usual process is for Gabriel, the proprietor of the pawn shop that never opens, to direct his would-be customers to Bailey's Café where the maestro helps them find Eve's if they know how to ask. But as Eve trims her camellias, she looks up to see Gabriel standing beside Mariam, requesting Eve to take her in. Gabriel breaks the pattern (145) because this woman is fourteen, pregnant, and "no man has ever touched [her]."

Gabriel's presence in Mariam's story repeats the biblical role Gabriel plays in Luke. As the messenger angel, he delivers surprising news "to a virgin betrothed to a man whose name was Joseph, of the house of David; and the virgin's name was Mary" (Luke 1:27); sensing her fear, he continues, "Do not be afraid, Mary, for you have found favor with God. And behold, you will conceive in your womb and bear a son, and you shall call his name Jesus" (Luke 1:30–31). After Gabriel's departure, Mary visits Elizabeth, who is carrying the one who will be John the Baptist, and Elizabeth sings praises to Mary and the unborn child: "Blessed are you among women, and blessed is the fruit of your womb!" (Luke 1:42). When Naylor's Gabriel delivers Mariam to Eve's doorstep, he turns away, and Mariam gives Eve a plum. As a symbol, the plum is the literal fruit of her own womb. And it is this plum that Eve takes to Bailey's Café, asking Nadine for a knife to cut out the pit. The process of Eve's surgery on the plum gives Nadine the shivers, while the talk continues into past time in Ethiopia. When Eve plunges the knife into the plum in order to remove the pit, it does not come out clean, but rather has "ragged pieces of dark amber flesh with it," and what is left of the delicate outer skin begins "to curl inward like a petal" (151). The removal of the pit suggests the removal of Mariam's baby. While the pit can be cleaned off, as can be the baby, the fruit surrounding that pit is wasted, used up, as is the mother. The plum functions as a powerful metaphor for the reader's visceral understanding of Mariam's situation.

Mariam is the first child of a Beta Israel mother, one of the Ethiopian Jews, "outcasts in their own nation" (146), who strictly follow Jewish traditions. Four unidentified biblical passages are cited in the midst of Mariam's mother's story, beginning with Deuteronomy 6:4–5 (146), closely followed by verses 6–7 (146) of the same chapter and book. The latter calls on the child's guardians to teach the child these ways, for they are commandments from their God. But through Mariam's mother's pain, the reader comes to understand a different interpretation of the dictates. Mariam's mother has delivered a female child, for which she must stay fourteen days in the "hot and airless hut of blood" (147), moving to a second hut for another sixty-six days because she is unclean (147). Naylor's language is a reminder of the law stated in Leviticus12:5. On the birth of a male child, the mother has only seven days, followed by thirty-three days that she shall be unclean (Leviticus

12:2, 4). The Beta Israel expect and look forward to the birth of sons, but Mariam's mother wants the female child, "tells no one how hard she begged Adonai" for the child to be female and secretly hopes that the second one will also be female (148). Mariam's mother wants the time away from her husband so that she can return more fully rested; male children reduce the rest time by half. Although Mariam's mother wants this to happen, she feels guilty because she is not following the letter of the law—all interpreted through Eve's understanding of how she believes Mariam's mother must have felt.

Circumcision is the subject of the third passage, Genesis 17:9–11 (147); part of God's covenant with Abraham is that every male child shall be circumcised. In Beta Israel this becomes the course of action for female children as well. While Mariam's mother had her purification when she was three, Mariam is over twice that age when her mother begins to plea for Mariam's. Nadine expresses her horror at the thought of the procedure, claiming "this *isn't* in the Law of Moses," but Eve's response is that "it's older than that. It's the law of the Blue Nile. And along those shores there is no woman in her right mind—Jew or Muslim—who will want her daughter to grow up a whore" (150). The discussion of female circumcision between Nadine and Eve remains in a nonjudgmental mode, considering the event within its historical and cultural contexts. Alice Walker's less successful 1992 novel *Possessing the Secret of Joy,* published the same year as *Bailey's Café,* drew popular attention to the subject of clitoridectomies, or more precisely, female genital mutilation. In Naylor's work, no blame is placed on the mother's decision, only unmitigated compassion for Mariam. As Nadine becomes "so angry [she] wanted to break something. Blame somebody," she notices that Eve has become quiet and that "ever so softly she was crying" (152). Eve is first woman; she has been around since the beginning, and this is enough to make her cry. Naylor's choice to make Eve's response so understated produces one of the most poignant moments in the novel.

The last scripture comes from Proverbs 31:10–12 (151–52), about a virtuous woman, whose price is far above rubies. Mariam's painful small opening (151) ironically raises a woman's value (152). But Mariam's mother's request that she be especially tight so that her menstrual blood can only make its way out drip by drip (151) actually prevents her from having intercourse with any man. As with her biblical counterpart, an immaculate conception again happens. She will bear a child even though no man has ever touched her.

Biblically, Gabriel appears to Mary; Mariam has made her way from Addis Ababa to Gabriel's pawn shop, where she finds "a white Falasha" (159). This term, considered derogatory today, comes from *filasi,* which means landless people, a reference to the defeat of the Jews.[36] Gabriel, who earlier has been identified as one who carries his birth "on his face" (145) and is placed in the Caucasus Mountains, which hold together the Black and Caspian Seas, most likely uses the term to suggest the Diaspora. Because Eve's place is meant to be a way station, both she and Nadine worry about where Mariam will return. It is late fall of 1948, and Israel has only been a Jewish state since May; Eve knows it would take time to make arrangements. But most pressing is the child that is coming. For the first time in the novel, Eve appears content not to read the future, but to wait.

## "Miss Maple's Blues"

The last of the seven characters who has a solo in the jam is a man. When he makes his way to Bailey's Café, he is "set on using the last money he had in his pocket to buy a pawnshop revolver" (165). On a crowded night in the café, the first person he meets is Eve, who hires him as her housekeeper. By the time the maestro is introduced to him, Stanley Beckwourth Booker T. Washington Carver (unidentified surname) has been dubbed Miss Maple by Eve. Along with Mariam, Miss Maple's introduction to the way station is not strictly according to process; but then Stanley is not exactly another woman whose story is mired in sexual degradation or abusive addiction. Stanley's is a story of racial discrimination and degradation, yet on the part of those who see him, a target for sexually pejorative name-calling.

He finds comfort from the heat in wearing women's dresses, "light percale housedresses most of the time" (163). He is carefully described so as not to be taken as a man who deliberately tries to pass as a woman. He makes no effort to camouflage his male body; women's dresses are simply a cooler alternative to his hot wool flannel interview suit. As a man with a Stanford Ph.D. in statistics and a hundred job rejections from every major city from the West to the East coast, he figures that the likelihood of securing a position in his field of expertise will not be altered by wearing a dress. The maestro goes to some lengths to remind Sugar Man and Jesse Bell, who call him a faggot (116), that Miss Maple is not a homosexual: "Come on, Miss Maple isn't a queer" (116) and for Sugar Man, "*faggot* has been the kindest thing he's called Miss Maple" (164).

Naylor's choice of having Eve call him Miss Maple suggests connections with Scott Joplin's popular 1899 "Maple Leaf Rag." A definition of *rag* itself—"the constant collision between internal melodic and underlying rhythms"[37]—supports Miss Maple's difficult position for an educated black man in 1940s America. Miss Maple's internal melody has a hard-won integrity, but as he moves into a white-dominated society to find challenging employment in his profession, he continues to collide with those underlying rhythms of a period of American history in which doors were shut simply because of skin color. The number of times he is turned down, while countable in Miss Maple's case, is representative of the legion of capable people that would generate the crisis that led to affirmative action legislation. Naylor makes a point of having Miss Maple's intention clearly stated. When one potential employer mumbles about the day "we'll bring ourselves to hire a Negro," Miss Maple's response shows common sense: "You'll be doing your company a better favor, . . . when you can bring yourself to hire the most qualified man" (197). The fact that Naylor does not substitute *person* for *man* reflects 1940s speech.

Miss Maple's background also addresses another race-related issue that is not explored among the other women. Stanley is mixed-race—Native-American, Hispanic, and African American, but he lived in California where his identity was crushed into "one six-letter word" (171). While his father, a highly successful businessman and land owner, could own a prestigious La Salle convertible and drive up to the local bank to conduct his financial transactions, he could not do so without incurring the rage of the white men in town: "He'd come back out of the bank to find all of his whitewalls flat and that six-letter word scrawled in mud over his windshield" (172). During his own adolescence, Stanley "thought [his] father was pathetic for never fighting back," and it would take him a bizarre encounter to "understand that [his] father was also teaching [him] something very special: how to be [his] own man" (173).

In each of Naylor's novels, the masterpieces of Western world literature make a significant contribution to the lives of her characters. Shakespeare's plays have a recurring presence. When Stanley is ready to leave home for college, his father has purchased for him a set of thirty-eight volumes of Shakespeare's plays, including the sonnets. It is the kind of gift that his father knows will only increase in value and importance to Stanley as he matures, a present his father is more excited to give than Stanley is ready to receive. They must pick up the books from the head clerk Peters at the freighting office, a Ku Klux Klan member, whose best side comes out when he sees the contents of the crates: "Peters opened the cover like a man making love and wiped his sweaty hands on his trousers before daring to touch the tissue overleaf" (177). Shakespeare has power in this brief moment to bring together a Klansman and a black man; each has a history with the other, yet this moment lets the other become aware of how much they do not know about each other: "And then each looked into the other's eyes, knowing what they were doing while knowing they couldn't stop" (177). Until the Gatlin boys appear on the scene, Peters and Stanley's father relate to each other as human-to-human, without the labels.

But the Gatlins' presence destroys what the Shakespeare collection had created. A fight ensues, and Stanley and his father wind up naked, locked in the storeroom. Still, Stanley's father holds firm to his integrity, for it means everything that he set an example for Stanley. The climax of this scene once again is Shakespeare inspired. When the books enter the fracas, Stanley's father interprets what must be done through Shakespeare's own writing. The enemy had gouged the silk cover, "torn out handfuls of pages, crushed what was left . . . , and then urinated on the whole thing" (183). He donned a "red taffeta with spaghetti straps and a huge circular skirt" (184) that was available in one of the boxes in the storeroom to cover his naked body, knowing that men like the Gatlins would "go straight for the balls" (184), and blasted through the locked door to have a word with a man who would destroy *The Tempest:* "*When my son left me to go out on his own, I wanted to give him the vision of such a brave new world. You pissed on that gift*" (186). It is Miranda's line in Shakespeare work; this "brave new world / That has such people in't!" (V.1.217–18) is a world of wonder and mankind is beauteous. Shakespeare's vision is akin to Stanley's father's, but the Gatlins have intruded and reshaped the brave new world. Nevertheless, Stanley has received the message finally and substantially from his father, for in that moment, he "filled [his] world" and Stanley "would have followed him, dressed like anything, bound for anywhere" (186).

Changing his major at Stanford from the more subjective courses to one where getting a high grade depended on objective evaluation, serving time in prison for being a conscientious objector during WWII, learning how to survive prison rape, returning for the completion of his advanced degree, and setting out to find suitable employment took every bit of the inner resources his father had instilled in him. When he reaches Pittsburgh and the Waco Glass and Tile company and runs into another black man who has allegedly made it in corporate America, he finally abandons hope. "Domestic marketing" wants Stanley to have lunch with "the second in command at layout and design," another black man, who is similar to Maxwell Smyth, the man who sells out completely to white America in *Linden Hills*. In this unnamed man, Stanley sees who he could become: one who is second in command when he is the only person in the department, one whose lobster bib stays spotless during an eating challenge, one who has no definite opinions on anything that matters, one who shreds his bib into tiny pieces. This telling encounter leaves him no alternative but to seek his own end, and finding the pawnshop he sees the arrow pointing to the squat little café where he meets Eve.

Miss Maple has been with Eve for two years, and he will leave with enough money from writing jingles for commercials to establish his own business. As the 1949 new year rings in, Miss Maple is in community with the maestro. His father grounded him internally, but it took Eve's place to give him the rest he needed, the affirmation to become "one of the freest men" the maestro has ever known (216). Whether he departs from Eve's in a pair of pants or in a dress, as Stanley or Miss Maple, it matters little, for he has played out his ragtime and come to understand his worth.

## "The Wrap"

As the jam concludes, a new year begins and the maestro comes front and center to wrap this song, but he is careful to remind the reader that life is not a song. If it were, then the reader could expect some resolution, "with a lot of happy endings to leave you feeling real good that you took the time to listen" (219). However, these are the stories of people's lives, taken down to a lower key (34), where stories get told honestly and deeply, under the surface (35). Since life here in the way station is only a moment in the transition period, the jams do not reflect the whole of their stories, for their lives will continue.

Two loose ends remain here in the final pages of the novel. One is the relationship of Gabriel to the maestro, the archangel Michael. Gabriel is presented as a Russian Jew and Michael as an American Negro. The two represent two separate voices who have different opinions on practically every subject and are not afraid to tell each other those positions. They speak from two separate backgrounds, have a world view that is shaped by their early years and the cultures out of which they come. Their biblical counterparts represent two levels of the hierarchy of angels, a design which leaves Gabriel second only to Michael,[38] a position that helps explain why Gabriel is on one side and Bailey's Café anchors the center of the relay team, the holding/healing place for people with broken dreams.

The second loose end is the delivery of Mariam's baby, which Eve handles. She recreates the Ethiopian hillside that is Mariam's home, and unlike the earlier moment with the plum, both baby and mother survive his birth. Because the event is a community experience with lights everywhere—even Esther is present in the corner—Naylor suggests that the miracle happens because of the force and support of the community's presence. When the baby arrives, everyone is present to celebrate the moment; the unexpected happens—Nadine hugs the maestro; Gabriel, Miss Maple, and the maestro dance; Jesse does the flamenco; Peaches sings; Esther smiles; and the whole community joins in song. Eve has created a space where Mariam can follow the laws of the Beta Israel, can rest as Leviticus dictates. And on the eighth day, there will be circumcision. Gabriel is present to handle this moment, but the community stands strong. Miss Maple and the maestro become honorary stand-ins for the Jews who are not present. The maestro has come to understand that what he values most in Gabriel's faith is that "nothing important can happen unless they're all in it together as a community" (227).

Naylor foregoes the happy ending in the wrap, but she lets the maestro give a hopeful ending. Mariam dies in the wall of water that she has created to bathe in, so her young son George will be raised an orphan, never knowing that on the occasion of his birth "the world lit up with lights" (228). Readers of *Mama Day* know what happens in this Christ figure's life, that George grows up strong, finds surrogate mother figures in Miranda and

Abigail Day and love with Cocoa, for whom he sacrifices his own life.

*Bailey's Café* is a pause in life. Naylor is perhaps suggesting that resolution to stories will come in what has been said before. As a collective, characters recur, stories continue, themes repeat. To end one place is really only to rest, to go back, to start anew, and as T. S. Eliot stated in "Little Gidding" from *Four Quartets:* "We shall not cease from exploration / And the end of all our exploring / Will be to arrive where we started / And know the place for the first time."

# CHAPTER SIX

# *The Men of Brewster Place*

For her fifth novel Gloria Naylor revisits the neighborhood of her first, with a shift of focus and point of view. *The Men of Brewster Place* was published by Hyperion in the spring of 1998. The first book gives depth and dimension to this one, although it stands capably on its own. Once again using the number seven, Naylor tells the individual stories of seven men in a format that is similar to the earlier work. All but one are familiar to the reader of *The Women of Brewster Place:* Ben, the janitor who sits sentinel on his garbage-can lid against the fence has been resurrected from his earlier death to narrate; Basil, Mattie Michael's only son, who skipped bail, displacing Mattie from her home of thirty years and sending her to Brewster Place; Eugene, who missed his daughter's funeral; Moreland T. Woods, the visiting preacher whose voice seduced Etta Mae before his hands and body could turn the promise into a reality; C. C. Baker, the leader of the gang that raped Lorraine and caused her death; and Abshu, Kiswana's boyfriend who loved her feet and Shakespeare. Only Brother Jerome is new to Brewster Place. While the women had earlier celebrated a triumphant sense of community in their block party, the men's gathering place is the barbershop, where signs of defeat and despair abound. The metaphorical day of *The Women of Brewster Place* is reversed here. For the men Brewster Place begins at "Dusk" and ends with the promise of "Dawn."

Naylor's epigraph has two parts: the first is a series of three questions in a Langston Hughes poem delivered by an individual male voice who wants to know why *his* loneliness, song, and dream should be "deferred overlong"?[1] Important is the singular voice instead of the community so present among Naylor's women. The poem's title demands an answer: "Tell me." Instead of supplying an answer, however, Naylor turns, in the second part of the epigraph, to a second short poem by Hughes, "A Christian Country," to make a statement about a distant and drunk God who should "fight / Like a man." The novel's characters reflect the spirit of lost and waste found in the poem.

As the novel opens, the time is dusk, the end of the day and, metaphorically and hopefully, the end of bad times for the men who live on Brewster Place. Ben tells the reader "it always feels like dusk on Brewster Place" (6). He appears to set the record straight. For all the men who stayed—some proud and some pitiful—"there was always a Her in his story" (8). The men on Brewster Place have been more positively affected by the women in their lives than have the women by the men. By novel's end in "Dawn," when all the stories have been told, Abshu is the good soldier who sits alone to wait for the dawn to come. Abshu is the one good man who has fought the fight that the poet Langston Hughes wanted for his languishing God—to "get up and fight / Like a man." As the novel closes, the God Hughes depicted has been restored to his biblical place, and Abshu prays the "Our Father, who art in heaven" that Jesus taught. When Willie and Lester, hand in hand, "walked out of Tupelo Drive into the last days of the year"[2] at the close of *Linden Hills,* they had each other. *The Men of Brewster Place* is a novel of men who do not share a common goal, a common dream; each is alone. Abshu is the concluding reminder of the men's isolation from each other: "he will leave this street to walk into a rising sun. One man against the dawning of the inevitable" (172).

## "Ben"

Ben is the closest figure to a surrogate father that exists for those who make their home on Brewster Place. He does not offer advice nor nurture Brewster's children, but his presence and his drinking are a constant. Perhaps the greatest gift from this 68-year-old man, who "aint never been in a situation where anybody ever called [him] sir" (11), is his willingness to listen. Embedded in Ben's story are three lessons that Ben learns for survival. The lessons then re-appear in the stories of Jerome, Basil, and Eugene.

Ben learns the first lesson early in his life: silence can mean survival. This lesson comes from Grandpa Jones. Ben has a memory of his grandfather "sitting in his porch rocker with a closed Bible in his lap" (12); he promises to open that Bible "when someone shows [him] the place that says white people is going to hell" (12). The story that closes the Bible permanently for Ben's grandfather is not spoken: "It was a story that he carried inside; because there was no words he could use to talk about silence" (13).

With a typeface switch to italics, Naylor moves the novel into memory. Grandpa Jones' story is too painful for words. As an old man, when he sits with his hand on that closed Bible, he physically manifests his intention to contain and continue the hatred that he feels for that long-ago solitary white man who beat, raped, and caused the death of his ten-year-old sister. When no words of injustice are spoken at her funeral, the brother who would become Ben's grandfather spoke the only words that would ever leave his mouth in the name of racial injustice. He knew as a child that the minister had been wrong. The Lord had not taken away Sister; the white man had. But when he yelled out to the minister, his mother slapped him. As a child, he got the first loud and clear message of black survival in a white world: "*Boy, shut your mouth, you hear? Shut your mouth. Be a man*" (15). Silence was not only expected but associated with manliness.

Ben learns the second lesson about how to behave in the world from the bellhop Billy. Billy's promotions up the hotel chain of opportunity—from emptying spittoons to bellhopping—were granted because he had a positive attitude about his work. What could be considered an eagerness simply to be the best that he could be at his various tasks was interpreted by his black male coworkers as being "a house Negro," and they "hated him" for his work ethic and his appearance (18). Whatever unstated pressures exist in Billy are unleashed by his fellow employee Rayburn when he "accidentally stepped on the toes of Billy's [brightly shined] shoes" (18), causing Billy to go berserk. Naylor does not overtly state why Billy snaps, but the reader understands through what Ben knows: "There wasn't a whole lot of work for black men like us outside of picking cotton; and some would do anything to keep from having to go back to the fields" (18). The white man's economic control of honest work is difficult enough—add to that the pressures of the black man's interpretation of someone's playing Uncle Tom to the white boss.

Ben moves on, armed with the knowledge of what he must do in this world. Both lessons teach isolation. He must be silent, and if he is "good" at his work, his male coworkers will hate him. The third lesson is twofold; from his daughter's experience with Mr. Clyde, the white man for whom he and Elvira are sharecroppers, he experiences firsthand an updated version of his grandfather's story—a young innocent black child-woman can be easily had by an older powerful white man and, as protector and father of his daughter, he is impotent to intervene. But the bottle becomes his temporary solace and escape when he is lacerated by Mr. Clyde. His "sweet girl" (21), his "baby" (22), rends his heart with the sad confession: "And when I told him . . . that I was gonna tell my daddy, all he did was laugh. He laughed. And laughed" (22–23). It is the recurring memory of this haunting laughter of the white man that becomes the impetus to get away from there. Eventually Ben finds his way to Brewster Place, but, as a black man, life has taught him he can never get away from "there." The answer to the familiar Shakespearean query—"So what does it mean to be a man?" (28)—is plaintive: keep silent, prepare to be hated, and when it matters most, expect derisive laughter.

## "Brother Jerome"

The solitary male character who does not appear in *The Women of Brewster Place* is a living example of the first of Ben's lessons, for Jerome does not speak. His function is to play "the black man's blues" (37). He is necessary among the men of Brewster Place because it his music with which the book will end; as Abshu leaves the street, "the music plays on . . . and on . . ." (173). Naylor's selection of *manchild,* claiming that "one manchild for the millenium" (173) is all that is needed, is a reminder of the source of the music, the manchild Jerome, whose "hands just got better and better while his mind stayed at three years old" (31–32).

Like Saint Jerome, who produced the *Vulgate,* the first authentic Latin translation of the Bible from Hebrew, Brother Jerome is also a translator, though his medium is different. For both Jeromes light plays an equally compelling role: for the historical Jerome a blinding light forced him from his delirium and into a renewed awareness of life,[3] for Brewster's Jerome light from the lamp magically leads the young Jerome to the piano. He has not ever played before, but through the light, by "listening for the light" (31), he somehow knows, without knowing, that he is telling the men of Brewster Place about their lives.

As the years pass his playing becomes holy work, for his blues receive "Amens" from apartments where individual men turn bitter about their lives. The stories stay individual, but the response to them becomes communal. Because no man speaks to another, the "Amens" come "from every brick; every piece of concrete and iron railing on Brewster Place" (37). When Naylor sends the "Amens" through inanimate objects, she heightens the isolation of men who have long been taught to remain silent.

## "Basil"

While Ben tells the story of Jerome, Basil speaks for himself. Though he is the cause of his mother's losing her home and moving to Brewster Place, he does not live on the street. By the time he has earned the money to repay his mother, Mattie Michael is dead. To pay honor to her, she having sacrificed in many ways her own life for his, he decides that he will "find some woman, somewhere, and make her life happy" (46). But first he has to find the father that he never knew.

Readers of *The Women of Brewster Place* know that Butch Fuller is not the marrying type and that he represents the single experience with sexual passion that Mattie ever knew. When Basil meets his father, he realizes that the moment that also produced his conception was his mother's solitary sexual experience. What Mattie never knew, however, is that Butch did know that she was pregnant, had tried to visit her, and was prevented from doing so by her father, "a hard, hard man" (48). What is particularly poignant is that Butch never asks Basil his name, yet he knows which name Mattie must have chosen for him. According to the first novel Basil is conceived on a field of basil—she pleaded with Butch to "do something—anything . . . before she burst . . . in a million pieces among the roots of the trees and the leaves of the tiny basil."[4] For Butch to call his son by the correct name is unexplained during the first and only conversation that father will have with son, but Butch's knowing suggests that his experience with Mattie also affected him, lived on in his memory.

Taking the one new piece of information that he learns from his father, that his own sperm count may be insufficient to fertilize an egg and produce the child that can make him the father he wants to be, Basil returns to the city to enter an understanding of the second lesson that Ben had learned: prepare to be hated. Basil has a history of womanizing, but once he declares his interest in commitment, women spurn him. Naylor suggests through Basil's progress toward a successful relationship that "black men weren't the only reason for the mess black women were in" (51).

Naylor duplicates the parenting role of Mattie in Basil's relationship with his sons. In his ultimate marriage to Keisha, he learns that placing fatherhood *before* a meaningful and loving relationship with his children's mother, who happens to be his wife, throws his pledge to make some woman happy off balance. When Basil commits his first loyalty to sons Jason and Eddie, he falls into the same life pattern that he watched his mother play out for him. And just as he runs out on Mattie and returns too late for her to know that her life choices did matter to him, a frustrated Keisha notifies authorities, who arrest him to pay for that outstanding warrant, which caused Mattie to lose her home. Six years later, when he attempts to reenter the lives of his sons—one who has done time in juvenile detention and the other who has "built a shell around himself" (64)—they do not know him. Though, as his mother would have done for him, he is determined to "fight like hell" to restore a relationship with his sons, he is doomed to live out his life never knowing if he "could have made a difference" (64) but having some real assurance, at least temporarily, that doing the right thing nets hatred from those whose opinions matter most.

## "Eugene"

Ben's introduction to Eugene's story prepares the careful reader for the unfolding of some mystery, perhaps one that is best left unexplored. Ben cannot figure out why Eugene keeps returning to Ceil,[5] but he knows that if he had taken the "*trouble to listen to Brother Jerome's blues as Eugene comes and goes, [he] would get the answer*"; however, the next line is essential: "*But that would be like peeking in through someone's bedroom window*" (68). When it is Eugene's turn to tell his story, Naylor has him explain himself to his erstwhile wife Ceil, who, at the end of her tragic tale in *The Women of Brewster Place,* leaves for San Francisco. What Eugene has to admit is too private to confess in a public forum; Ceil is the only one who deserves to hear it, and the only safe way to unload the complexity of his feelings is to speak to Ceil in her absence.

Through Eugene the reader hears more of Ceil's story. Because the two have known each other from the time they were fourteen and twelve, respectively, his story is entangled in hers. His inability to talk about his preference for men addresses the third lesson that Ben had to learn: when something matters most, expect derisive laughter. The word that identifies Eugene is centered in the middle of a line by itself in italics—*faggot* (70, 72, 74, 82)—as though the word itself interrupts his telling, just as the reality of the word interrupts his life; the word's position suggests that Eugene does not speak the word. Confusing for Eugene is his sincere and all-encompassing love for Ceil and the simultaneous guilt that he carries because he knows that he "proceeded slowly, very slowly, to ruin [her] life" (71).

The part of the day that changes his life starts with a one-on-one basketball game with Bruce, his foreman on the docks, and the chilling awareness without spoken words—"watching the ball make that perfect arch from his hands to the hoop, it came to [him]: he knows" (75). Naylor collapses time from a moment in the basketball game when both men go up "past the old rusted hoop" to when they land "on two corner stools near the window at the Bull & Roses in the financial district" (78). The Bull & Roses is the same gay bar that Eugene had tried to enter on earlier occasions by himself, but he could never screw his courage to the sticking place and open the door. Bruce is the example of a man comfortable in his choices, indifferent to what the world knows or thinks of him. Eugene is the opposite—scared, confident only in his thoughts that Ceil will see a freak. Since he decides he knows Ceil's thoughts, there is no reason to explain himself truthfully; he has to find refuge in the lies that will grow from small to big. And the confusion remains: he loves Ceil "so much, it hurts," while at the same time he also knows that when he "went home with another man . . ., it felt so complete" (84). Eugene could not sustain consistency in either lifestyle—unspoken dissatisfaction with Ceil drives him to men, who, in turn, cause him to feel guilt so profound for hurting Ceil that he returns to her.

His coming and going might have continued, but his daughter's death permanently causes the break. Naylor records in her first novel Ciel's painful journey back to sanity after Serena dies. Ciel is surrounded by a community of women who will not abandon her; however, Eugene has no one. He is left to the donning of masks to hide his pain, his despair. Fearing he will kill himself, Eugene seeks redemption. Since he feels God has abandoned him, he turns to the one who was "his own god" (79), the one who offered himself as Eugene's "fairy godmother" (85). When he knocks on Chino's door, Eugene does not need to offer more than "they buried my baby today" (93) to have Chino understand that Eugene "had come for redemption" (94). The leather whip that Chino reaches for is a cat-o'-nine-tails.[6] Naylor links her description of the whip with a Roman scourge—the kind that Jesus carried with him when he cleaned out the temple (John 2:15) and that Pilate used on the back of Jesus (John 19:1) before he washed his hands of the Crucifixion.[7] When Eugene "assume[s] the position" (94) and Chino begins the lashing that sends Eugene's blood flying to all parts of the gray-tiled room, he suffers the pain that Jesus had endured. Jesus went from a scourging to the cross; Eugene's last lines encourage Chino not to stop the punishment. If Eugene does not die from his effort at this moment of "redemption," the reader senses that he will repeatedly return to Chino for subsequent floggings, searching always to pay enough for his role in Ceil's pain and Serena's death.

## "Moreland T. Woods"

Ben introduces the Reverend Woods, minister of Sinai Baptist, as one whose "*soul's been greased with Vaseline and nothing much really sticks there, nothing much is real*" (98).

Moreland T. Woods is a visitor to Brewster Place, not one of its sons. When he makes his appearance in Naylor's first novel, it is as a visiting preacher to Canaan Baptist. Here, the reader learns Woods has been the minister at Sinai Baptist for twelve years, the same church that the imbibing Rev. Michael T. Hollis served in Naylor's second novel, *Linden Hills.* Woods does not tell his own story; rather, a third-person narrator moves the story back and forth between Woods and his nemesis, Deacon Bennett, one of Brewster's own, who understands the importance of having "God's House . . . beautiful, solid" (105).

As Ben explains, Woods is slick—from his good looks, assisted by his fancy clothes and car, to his silver-tongued ability to intone a sermon that slides from his mouth to land safely in the hearts and heads of his congregation. As his "M.T." initials predict, Naylor draws a superficial Woods who has much in common with her earlier preacher-character Hollis, the one apparently from whom Woods inherits Sinai Baptist. Both ministers have strong grandmothers in their youths. Both have received a clear call to the ministry, which counters their playboy lifestyles yet does not stop their flirtatious attraction to other women after they marry. Readers know from *Linden Hills* that Sinai, under Hollis, is a wealthy, dried-up, spiritless church. When the Woodses become regular members of Sinai, they see "a church that needs a leader"; it is "never filled to more than half capacity" (104). Now that Woods has resurrected its life, he wants a larger church to serve as a springboard from which to launch his political career.

Ben makes clear, as well, that people on Brewster Place take seriously "*their children and their religion*" (97). As a resident of the neighborhood, Deacon Bennett understands this better than Sinai's preacher. Sinai was "*his* church . . .; he had even helped to build it—laid the cornerstone of the foundation and kept at it with the others—brick by brick" (105). For men down on their luck, which was often the case on Brewster Place, the church became a haven where men "became somebody, at the least, a child of God" (106). It was in the church, on the deacons' board, that Bennett could gain a stature that the world denied him. It was a place where he could assert his power, even against the successes of a popular preacher. Bennett will be at Sinai for life; Woods is temporary.

Bennett is willing to enter what Woods clearly sees as a game. For Brewster Place, Bennett wants the church to stay as it is; for himself Woods wants the church to support a building expansion. As the control of the congregation volleys between Bennett and Woods, the minister prevails, and the church expands. With the smooth soul that Ben has identified, Woods becomes a means by which Brewster Place members of Sinai can measure their own ragged wounds of the soul. Sinai will continue because people like Deacon Bennett will never stop fighting for it. Moreland T. Woods, on the other hand, is only passing through.

## "C. C. Baker"

C. C. Baker's role in *The Women of Brewster Place* is memorable for its marked violence in his leadership in the gang rape of Lorraine. He becomes one of "the most dangerous species in existence—human males with an erection to validate in a world that was only six feet wide."[8] No conclusion, no just retribution for his heinous crime against Lorraine, is part of C. C. Baker's story in *The Men of Brewster Place*. C. C. has gone on to another chapter in his life, which his father has predicted will end in "the graveyard or the jail" (122). In present time C. C. Baker is being questioned by two police detectives who want to know his role in the shooting death of his stepbrother, Hakim. The narrative is composed solely of quick dialogue with no descriptions of any of the characters, the room where the official inquiry takes place, or the circumstances that have led to C. C.'s being interrogated.

The interrupting italicized paragraphs provide the substantive commentary which places C. C.'s life in a context that helps the reader understand his means of survival in the world. Ben does not narrate the rest of C. C.'s story; rather, the voice is C. C.'s articulate and insightful alter ego. This voice recognizes that C. C.'s vocabulary is limited to fifty words, with half of them being "some variation on the word, *fuck*" (121). It is a vocabulary that speaks volumes on the streets, the only place that can offer him those components his father has been denied: "*money, power, and respect*" (123).

In C. C.'s story Naylor indicates through the italicized paragraphs the all-powerful lure of the streets. A completely different code of honor exists here, and, to be part of that elite group, tests have to be passed. To win, to become a man, involves taking a magnum from under a coat and aiming "*for the face so he won't have to see his brother's eyes as he dies*" (129). The six-foot-wide world, the width of an alley in Naylor's first novel, is expanded by having success on the streets.

Killing a brother (only a stepbrother) or raping a woman (only a lesbian) is the way to be a winner, to be a man.

## "Abshu"

Of all the men of Brewster Place, Abshu is the most positive, the best role model for the generation that follows. Such was the case for Abshu in *The Women of Brewster Place* as Kiswana's supportive boyfriend, and in this novel Naylor enhances the earlier portrayal by supplying background that establishes Abshu's heartfelt connection to Brewster Place and its community center. Ben introduces Cliff Jackson to the reader by calling attention to his apparent birth name, to his desire to be called "Abshu," and to his own name, Benjamin— "but I've been called Ben all my life" (134)—which he determines has made no difference in how his life has turned out. By focusing the discussion on naming, Naylor does direct attention to Abshu's full birth name: Clifford Montgomery Jackson. His middle and last names are the capitals of two southern states— Alabama and Mississippi—but more to the point the sites of much civil rights activity, places where African American people made repeated stands against injustices. Now as Abshu, Jackson continues the fight against injustice—from "plotting the assassination of the Reverend Moreland Woods" (134) for betraying the residents of Brewster Place as soon as they helped secure his seat on the city council to teaching the young neighborhood boys how "to curse like Shakespeare did" (141).

As head of the community center, Abshu becomes the big supportive brother who provides younger boys, especially, a safe environment and entertainment that lead them to "see what the world had waiting" (136). In the community center he tries to create the kind of place that would have made a difference in his early years, back when his stone cold sober father took fists to his mother and he would pray, in his ironic world, that his father would come home drunk. Now Moreland T. Woods, first black man on the city council, by his betrayal in his first vote threatens the survival of both neighborhood and livelihood. It takes the shrewd lawyer friend B.B. Rey to plan the pregnant women's march on the city council meeting sufficiently to embarrass Woods and cause the council to ask for his resignation. Woods' womanizing, alluded to in passing in his story in this novel, is explored more fully in his evening with Etta Mae Johnson in Naylor's first novel. In Naylor's depiction of Abshu's home life and his later foster care and in her suggestion of Woods' moral abandonment of familial responsibility and the good-natured ribbing of B.B. Rey's seduction of multiple women, she runs the gamut of the difficulties that women both tolerate and perpetuate. The focus, however, for Abshu is on the children, the consequences for them in a world not of their making.

Naylor uses Shakespeare more broadly with Abshu than in her earlier novels. The young boy Sammy, whom Abshu teaches to curse with Shakespearean lines, along with Sammy's friends, is most likely the son of Brewster Place's Cora Lee, the woman who enjoys making babies in the dark with shadows that haunt her apartment. In *The Women of Brewster Place,* Cora Lee complains that in the park "somebody gave Sammy a reefer," and she worries that she could "end up with a bunch of junkies on [her] hands."[9] Abshu provides the only community deterrent to that happening. When he teaches the boys to fight with Shakespeare's words, Abshu roams freely among *The Merchant of Venice, All's Well That Ends Well, The Tempest, A Midsummer Night's Dream, Hamlet, Henry V, Othello, King Lear, Timon of Athens, Coriolanus,* and ends with a rousing rebuff from *Henry IV, Part 1:* "You starvelling, you eel-skin, you dried neat's tongue, you bull's pizzle, you stock-fish—Oh for breath to utter what is like thee!—you tailor's yard, you sheath, you bow-case, you vile standing *tuck!*" (II.4.245–248). Shakespeare's words are said by Falstaff as he recounts to Prince Hal his earlier skirmish with the presumed enemy, not realizing until he is told that the "enemy" is really the prince himself. The prince's response could well be Abshu's counsel: "Well, breathe awhile, and then to it again." Naylor's choice of these lines from Falstaff to his prince and one-day king are appropriate, as Sammy's target is not really the enemy; Billy and his crowd are youths whose lives probably have more similarities than not with his verbal rousters. Abshu turns to literature for help because he "believed there was something in Shakespeare for everyone" (135), but at the rout of Moreland Woods he hoped that "his work was making a difference" (154), an objective that Basil also hoped to live long enough to ascertain.

## "The Barbershop"

At the conclusion of *The Women of Brewster Place,* Mattie Michael has a troubling dream about the block party which precedes the event itself. In the dream, however, the women come together in a triumphant razing of the wall, while "all of the men and children . . . stood huddled in the doorways" out of the rain.[10] It is the women, in the dream, who collectively take control of the neighborhood that has been their home. In *The Men of Brewster Place* what communal spirit exists has its "heartbeat . . . at Max's place" (157), the old-fashioned barbershop where men gather to solve "every problem in the world before the shop closes each day" (158). The problems they focus on, however, are never local or personal; rather, they are global and generic: "white men, black men, and women" (158). Max's place is a space for speaking the blues that Brother Jerome plays, only his music is more intimate because there are no words. Talk comes easy here precisely because it is detached, removed from each man's private world.

Greasy changes the unwritten rules of the shop. Although he repeats his two lines—"I'm trying" and "I'm a man" (160, 161, 165, 166)—the action that demonstrates his understanding of what those words mean is to first grab barber Henry and hold a straight razor to his throat. Because he is a man, he can let Henry go, but that same knowledge, even though crack has been "eating away at his brains" (159), causes him to define his manliness by slitting his own throat. As the blood gushes all over the mirrors and every man in the shop, Greasy's message is disturbing at a profoundly deep level. The men's marked surprise and their impotence to stop the self-inflicted death have to be handled privately, for even when Max's reopens a week after Greasy's death, no one speaks of that event. Each knew that he had contributed to the act, each had used Greasy "for the garbage can to hold all [their] fears" (167). After Greasy's death, though, the barbershop becomes even more important. As Ben claims, it is the place "to look into each others' eyes and see what we need to see . . . we thrive and are alive" (167). Because the reader has Ben's perception of the world in the barbershop, the knowledge of men's connection is in their looking at each other; no words are spoken. Language, so important in the community of women, appears to diminish men's lives. What Ben has learned early in his life still holds as Brewster Place moves toward "Dawn"—silence is survival.

But Naylor leaves Ben's message behind, a relic of a passing day. The closing image does not linger in the past but has an eye to the future. Abshu embodies a hope that will be found in language: "a million voices raised to a roar to say, No, this should not be" (172). Abshu walks out of this metaphorical day toward dawn, "as the music plays on . . . and on" (173), with the promise that the man of tomorrow will be redefined through articulate spoken language. The men are not a community, but as long as there is one Abshu, the dream can live on.

## Chapter One: Understanding Gloria Naylor

1. "Gloria Naylor," *I Know What the Red Clay Looks Like,* ed. Rebecca Carroll (New York: Crown, 1994) 160.

2. Donna Perry, ed., "Gloria Naylor," *Backtalk: Women Writers Speak Out* (New Brunswick, N.J.: Rutgers University Press, 1993) 222.

3. "Women of Brewster Place," *Ebony* 44 (Mar. 1989): 123.

4. "Black Women Novelists: New Generation Raises Provocative Issues," *Ebony* 40 (Nov. 1984): 64.

5. Naylor, *Bailey's Café* (New York: Harcourt Brace Jovanovich, 1992) 4. All parenthetical citations from *Bailey's Café* are from this edition.

6. Naylor, "Reflections," *Centennial,* ed. Michael Rosenthal (New York: Pindar Press, 1986) 71.

7. James W. Silver, *Mississippi: The Closed Society* (New York: Harcourt, Brace & World, 1966) 6–10.

8. "Gloria Naylor," *World Authors 1980–1985,* ed. Vineta Colby (New York: H. W. Wilson, 1991) 636.

9. Virginia Woolf, *A Room of One's Own* (New York: Harcourt Brace Jovanovich, 1929) 27.

10. "Graceful Passages," *Essence* 21 (May 1990): 136.

11. Naylor and Toni Morrison, "A Conversation," *Southern Review* 21 (July 1985): 568.

12. Perry, *Backtalk* 225.

13. J.R. Moehringer, "Keeping Up with the Characters," *New York Times Book Review* 21 Feb. 1988: 7.

14. Perry, *Backtalk* 230.

15. Perry, *Backtalk* 225.

16. Pearl Cleage, "Gloria Naylor," *Catalyst* Summer 1988: 57.

## Chapter Two: *The Women of Brewster Place*

1. Gloria Naylor, "Mama Still Loves You," *Redbook* 172 (Dec. 1988): 42+.

2. Gloria Naylor, "A Life on Beekman Place," *Essence* 11 (Mar. 1980): 82+.

3. Gloria Naylor, "When Mama Comes to Call . . .," *Essence* 13 (Aug. 1982): 67+.

4. Bill Katz and Linda Sternberg Katz, eds. *Magazines for Libraries* (New Providence, N.J.: R.R. Bowker, 1995) 1159.

5. Katz and Katz, 1163.

6. Dorothy Wickenden, "*The Women of Brewster Place*," *New Republic* 187 (6 Sept. 1982): 37–38.

7. Annie Gottlieb, "Women Together," *New York Times Book Review* 22 Aug. 1982: 11, 25.

8. Loyle Hairston, "A Good First Shot," *Freedomways* 23 (Fourth Quarter 1983): 284.

9. Hairston, 285.

10. Langston Hughes, *The Collected Poems,* ed. Arnold Rampersad (New York: Alfred A. Knopf, 1994) 387.

11. James A. Emanuel, *Langston Hughes* (New York: Twayne, 1967) 149.

12. Gloria Naylor, *The Women of Brewster Place* (New York: Viking, 1982) 192. All further parenthetical citations from *The Women of Brewster Place* are from this edition.

13. Mrs. C.F. Leyel, *The Magic of Herbs: A Modern Book of Secrets* (New York: Harcourt, Brace, 1926) 110.

14. On the hot day in July 1996 when I visited the community of Rockvale, I got out of the car to the sound of chickens pecking and shuffling. I was immediately reminded of a young Mattie in her front yard feeding the biddies. The man with whom I spoke in the Rockvale Store was a long-time resident of the area and remembered when sugar

cane grew there and is the source for affirming that the Morgans were large property owners in the area.

15. Susan Meisenhelder, "'Eating Cane' in Gloria Naylor's *The Women of Brewster Place* and Zora Neale Hurston's 'Sweat,'" *Notes on Contemporary Literature* 23 (Mar. 1993): 5–7.

16. Toni Morrison, *Beloved* (New York: Signet, 1991) 335.

17. Joyce Elaine King and Carolyn Ann Mitchell, *Black Mothers to Sons: Juxtaposing African American Literature with Social Practice* (New York: Peter Lang, 1995) 9,11.

18. John D'Emilio and Estelle B. Freedman, *Intimate Matters: A History of Sexuality in America* (New York: Harper & Row, 1988) 101.

19. D'Emilio and Freedman, 101.

20. For further exploration of this topic, see Lillian Smith, *Killers of the Dream* (New York: Norton, 1978), especially "Three Ghost Stories," 114–37.

21. James Robert Saunders, *The Wayward Preacher in the Literature of African American Women* (Jefferson, N.C.: McFarland, 1995) 108.

22. Stuart Nicholson, *Billie Holiday* (Boston: Northeastern University Press, 1995) 196.

23. Nicholson, 232.

24. *The Ultimate Jazz Fakebook,* Comp. Herb Wong (Milwaukee: Hal Leonard, 1988) 131.

25. H. Nigel Thomas, *From Folklore to Fiction: A Study of Folk Heroes and Rituals in the Black American Novel* (New York: Greenwood Press, 1988) 43.

26. Charles V. Hamilton, *The Black Preacher in America* (New York: William Morrow & Co., 1972) 1.

27. The name Kiswana does not appear in the following name books: Chief Osuntoki, *The Book of African Names* (Baltimore: Black

Classic Press, 1971); Molefi Kete Asante, *Book of African Names* (Trenton, N.J.: Africa World Press, 1991); Julia Stewart, *African Names* (Secaucus, N.J.: Citadel Press, 1993); Elza Dinwoodie-Boyd, *Proud Heritage: 11,001 Names for Your African-American Baby* (New York: Avon, 1994). In the latter book, the closest name to Kiswana is Kizuwanda, listed under African Names for Girls, meaning, from Zaramo, "the last born."

28. Robert L. Chapman, ed., *New Dictionary of American Slang* (New York: Harper & Row, 1986) 81.

29. Derek Elley, ed. *Variety Movie Guide* (New York: Prentice Hall, 1992) 539, 587.

30. Usha Bande, "Murder as Social Revenge in *The Street* and in *The Women of Brewster Place,*" *Notes on Contemporary Literature* 23 (Jan. 1993): 5.

## Chapter Three: *Linden Hills*

1. Gloria Naylor, *Linden Hills* (New York: Ticknor & Fields, 1985) 1. All parenthetical citations from *Linden Hills* are from this edition.

2. Toni Morrison, *Sula* (New York: Bantam, 1973) 4.

3. Mel Watkins, "The Circular Driveways of Hell," *New York Times Book Review* 3 Mar. 1985: 11.

4. Sherley Anne Williams, "Roots of Privilege: New Black Fiction," *Ms.* June 1985: 70.

5. Joseph A. Brown, "With Eyes like Flames of Fire," *Callaloo* 8 (Spring–Summer 1985): 484–85.

6. Joe Johnson, "Books," *The Crisis* 92 (May 1985): 13.

7. Sam Cornish, "Middle-Class Souls on Ice," *Christian Science Monitor Book Review* 1 Mar. 1985: B1.

8. Roz Kaveney, "Solutions to Dissolutions," *TLS* 24 May 1985: 572.

9. Ernst and Johanna Lehner, *Folklore and Symbolism of Flowers, Plants and Trees* (New York: Tudor Publishing, 1960) 69.

10. Jupiter Hammon, "An Address to Miss Phillis Wheatly [*sic*], Ethiopian Poetess, in Boston, who came from Africa at eight years of age, and soon became acquainted with the gospel of Jesus Christ," *The Heath Anthology of American Literature,* vol.1, ed. Paul Lauter et al., (Lexington, Mass.: D. C. Heath, 1990) 685.

11. Sondra A. O'Neale, *Jupiter Hammon and the Beginnings of African-American Literature* (Metuchen, N.J.: Scarecrow Press, 1993) 2.

12. Dante Alighieri, *The Divine Comedy: The Inferno,* trans. Charles Singleton, (Princeton: Princeton University Press, 1970) 25.

13. Henry Louis Gates, Jr., "Significant Others," *Contemporary Literature* 29 (Winter 1988): 608.

14. George Breitman, ed., *Malcolm X Speaks* (New York: Grove Press, 1966) 1.

15. *The Inferno,* Canto V, 47.

16. Matthew Arnold, "Dante and Beatrice," *Essays in Criticism* (Boston: Ball Publishing, 1910) 93–94.

17. *The Inferno,* Canto II, 17.

18. *The Inferno,* Canto VIII, 83.

19. *The Inferno,* Canto I, 5, 7.

20. *The Inferno,* Canto IV, 43.

21. *The Inferno,* Canto V, 49.

22. *The Inferno,* Canto V, 57.

23. Gay Wilson Allen, *The Solitary Singer: A Critical Biography of Walt Whitman* (New York: New York University Press, 1967) 256.

24. "Cuisine Bourgeoise" first appeared in Stevens' 1942 *Parts of the World* collection. The poem, in its entirety, can be found in *Collected Poems of Wallace Stevens* (New York: Alfred A. Knopf, 1955) 227–28.

25. See Hanna Wallinger, "Gloria Naylor's *Linden Hills:* The

Novel by an African American Woman Writer and the Critical Discourse," *Moderne Sprachen* 37 (1993): 178.

26. Lillian Eichler, *The Customs of Mankind* (New York: Nelson Doubleday, 1924) 240–42.

## Chapter Four: *Mama Day*

1. Gloria Naylor, *Linden Hills* (New York: Ticknor & Fields, 1985) 147–48.

2. Gloria Naylor, *Mama Day* (New York: Ticknor & Fields, 1988) 1. All parenthetical citations from *Mama Day* are from this edition.

3. Missy Dehn Kubitschek, "Toward a New Order: Shakespeare, Morrison, and Gloria Naylor's *Mama Day*," *MELUS* 19 (Fall 1994): 77, 76.

4. Faith Pullin, "Acts of Reclamation," *TLS* (3–9 June 1988): 623.

5. Laurence Hull, "Review of *Mama Day*," *Library Journal* 113 (15 Feb. 1988): 179.

6. Patricia Olson, "Gloria Naylor's Unrealized Myth," *Christian Century* 105 (16 Nov. 1988): 1048.

7. "Review of *Mama Day*," *Kirkus Review* 55 (15 Dec. 1987): 1695.

8. Bharati Mukherjee, "There Are Four Sides to Everything," *New York Times Book Review* 21 Feb. 1988: 7.

9. Rosellen Brown, "*Mama Day*," *Ms.* 16 (Feb. 1988): 74.

10. Martha Southgate, "Love's Labors," *Village Voice* 33 (15 Mar. 1988) 52.

11. James Haskins, *Witchcraft, Mysticism and Magic in the Black World* (Garden City, N.Y.: Doubleday, 1974) 33.

12. Haskins, 77.

13. Haskins, 78.

14. Assurance that Naylor intended George as her Christ figure comes with a retelling of his mother's life in her fourth novel, *Bailey's Café*. See Chapter Five.

15. See Trudier Harris, "The Eye as Voice and Ear: African Southern Orality and Folklore in Gloria Naylor's *Mama Day*," in *The Power of the Porch: The Storyteller's Craft in Zora Neale Hurston, Gloria Naylor, and Randall Kenan* (Athens: University of Georgia Press, 1996) for her observation about justifiable killing (71) and the connection between Mrs. Jackson's handling of the sodomist in George's orphanage and Mama Day's fierce desire to protect her family.

16. Virginia C. Fowler, *Gloria Naylor: In Search of Sanctuary* (New York: Twayne, 1996) 113.

## Chapter Five: *Bailey's Café*

1. Gloria Naylor, *Mama Day* (New York: Ticknor & Fields, 1988) 131.

2. Gay Wilentz, "Healing the Wounds of Time," *The Women's Review of Books* 10 (Feb. 1993): 16.

3. Roz Kaveney, "At the Magic Diner," *TLS* 17 July 1992: 20.

4. Dan Wakefield, "'Noboby Comes in Here with a Simple Story,'" *New York Times Book Review* 4 Oct. 1992: 11.

5. Marie Jones, "Review of *Bailey's Café*," *Library Journal* 117 (1 Sept. 1992): 215.

6. Wilentz, "Healing the Wounds of Time," 16.

7. Thomas Jackson, "*Bailey's Café*," *America* 13 Feb. 1993: 18–19.

8. Ben Brantley, "A Gathering Place for Hope and Despair," *The New York Times* 14 Apr. 1994: C17.

9. Ralph Ellison, "Richard Wright's Blues," *Shadow and Act* (New York: Random House, 1964) 78–79.

10. Don Michael Randel, ed., *The New Harvard Dictionary of Music* (Cambridge, Mass.: Harvard University Press, 1986) 413.

11. Gloria Naylor, *Bailey's Café* (New York: Harcourt Brace Jovanovich, 1992) 76. All parenthetical citations from *Bailey's Café* are from this edition.

12. Randel, *Dictionary of Music* 902.

13. Naylor, *Mama Day* 131.

14. Mark Ribowsky, *A Complete History of The Negro Leagues 1884–1955* (New York: Carol Publishing, 1995) 21–22.

15. Robert Peterson, *Only the Ball Was White* (Englewood Cliffs, N.J.: Prentice-Hall, 1970) 3–4.

16. Ribowsky, *The Negro Leagues* 53

17. Peterson, *Only the Ball* 216–18.

18. Peterson, *Only the Ball* 74, 79.

19. Langston Hughes, *Famous Negro Heroes of America* (New York: Dodd, Mead, 1958) 183–86.

20. Hughes, *Famous Negro Heroes* 119–28.

21. *The Essential Duke Ellington* (New York: Amsco, 1995) 34–35.

22. Claire Powell, *The Meaning of Flowers: A Garland of Plant Lore & Symbolism from Popular Custom and Literature* (Boulder: Shambhala, 1979) 75.

23. Naylor, *Mama Day* 136.

24. Gloria Naylor, "Until Death Do Us Part," *Essence* 16 (May 1985): 133.

25. Leonard Gettelson, compiler, *Official World Series Records: 1903–1972* (St. Louis: *Sporting News,* 1972) 164, 166.

26. Joseph C. Goulden, *Mencken's Last Campaign: H. L. Mencken on the 1948 Election* (Washington, D.C.: New Republic Book Co., 1976) 9.

27. Powell, *The Meaning of Flowers* 92.

28. Ron Lackmann, *Same Time . . . Same Station: An A–Z Guide to Radio from Jack Benny to Howard Stern* (New York: Facts On File, 1996) 245.

29. Powell, *The Meaning of Flowers* 118.

30. H. L. Binsse, trans., *Mary Magdalene,* by Raymond-Leopold Bruckberger (New York: Pantheon: 1953) 17, 28.

31. Barry Kernfeld, ed., *New Grove Dictionary of Jazz* (New York: St. Martin's Press, 1996) 876.

32. Robert L. Crowell, *The Lore & Legends of Flowers* (New York: Thomas Y. Crowell, 1982) 13.

33. Harold Wentworth and Stuart Berg Flexner, eds., *Dictionary of American Slang,* 2nd ed. (New York: Thomas Y. Crowell, 1975) 361, 146.

34. Samuel B. Charters and Leonard Kunstadt, *Jazz: A History of the New York Scene* (New York: Da Capo, 1981) 188, 186.

35. Crowell, *Lore & Legends of Flowers* 57, 61.

36. Susan Hattis Rolef, ed. *Political Dictionary of the State of Israel,* 2nd ed. (New York: MacMillan, 1993) 102.

37. Stanley Sadie, ed., *The New Grove Dictionary of Music and Musicians,* vol. 15 (Washington, D.C.: MacMillan, 1980) 537.

38. Paul J. Achtemeier, ed. *Harper's Bible Dictionary* (San Francisco: Harper & Row, 1985) 326.

## Chapter Six: *The Men of Brewster Place*

1. Gloria Naylor, *The Men of Brewster Place* (New York: Hyperion, 1998) epigraph page. All parenthetical citations for *The Men of Brewster Place* are from this edition.

2. Gloria Naylor, *Linden Hills* (New York: Ticknor & Fields, 1985) 304.

3. Quoted in Jean Steinmann, *Saint Jerome and His Times,* trans, Ronald Matthews (Notre Dame, Ind.: Fides, 1959) 40.

4. Naylor, *The Women of Brewster Place* 17.

5. Naylor alters the spelling of "Ceil" in this novel. When she appears in the first novel, her name is spelled "Ciel."

6. Thomas Muray and Thomas Murrell, *The Language of Sado-masochism: A Glossary and Linguistic Analyses* (New York: Greenwood Press, 1989) 49.

7. Melancthon Jacobus, Edward Nourse, and Andrew Zenos, eds. *A New Standard Bible Dictionary* (New York: Funk & Wagnalls, 1926) 814.

8. Naylor, *The Women of Brewster Place* 170.

9. Naylor, *The Women of Brewster Place* 118.

10. Naylor, *The Women of Brewster Place* 185.

# BIBLIOGRAPHY

## Books by Gloria Naylor

*The Women of Brewster Place.* New York: Viking Press, 1982. London: Hodder and Stoughton, 1983. Novel.

*Linden Hills.* New York: Ticknor & Fields, 1985. London: Hodder and Stoughton, 1985. Novel.

*Mama Day.* New York: Ticknor & Fields, 1988. London: Hutchinson, 1988. Novel.

*Bailey's Café.* New York: Harcourt Brace Jovanovich, 1992. London: Heinemann, 1992. Novel.

Editor, *Children of the Night: The Best Short Stories by Black Writers, 1967 to the Present.* Boston: Little, Brown, 1996.

*The Men of Brewster Place.* New York: Hyperion, 1998. Novel.

## Selected Periodical Appearances by Gloria Naylor

"Eva McKinney—A Life of Toil, a Triumph of Spirit: Reminiscences of the Old South." *People* 23 (11 Mar. 1985): 86–88+.

"Finding Our Voice." *Essence* 26 (May 1995): 193.

"Graceful Passages." *Essence* 21 (May 1991): 136.

"Hers." *New York Times* 30 Jan. 1986: C2. (on *Wheel of Fortune*)

"Hers." *New York Times* 6 Feb. 1986: C2. (on dating)

"Hers." *New York Times* 13 Feb. 1986: C2. (on psychics)

"Hers." *New York Times* 20 Feb. 1986: C2. (on the spoken word)

"A Life on Beekman Place." *Essence* 11 (Mar. 1980): 82+.

"Love and Sex in the Afro-American Novel." *Yale Review* 78 (Autumn 1988): 19–31.

"Mama Still Loves You." *Redbook* 172 (Dec. 1988): 42+.

"Message to Winston." *Essence* 13 (Nov. 1982): 78–81.

"Myth of the Matriarch." *Life* 11 (Spring 1988): 65.

"Reflections." *Centennial.* Edited by Michael Rosenthal. New York: Pindar Press, 1986. 68–71.

"Sexual Ease." *Essence* 19 (Dec. 1988): 108.

"A Silent Night." *New York Times Magazine* 20 Dec. 1992: 14.

"Until Death Do Us Part." *Essence* 16 (May 1985): 133.

"When Mama Comes to Call. . . ." *Essence* 13 (Aug. 1982): 67+.

## Selected Interviews, Conversations, and Panels with Gloria Naylor

Cleage, Pearl. "Gloria Naylor." *Catalyst* Summer 1988: 56–59.

Denison, D. C. "Gloria Naylor." *Boston Globe Magazine* 13 Feb. 1994: 7.

Epel, Naomi, ed. "Gloria Naylor." *Writers Dreaming.* New York: Carol Southern Books, 1993, 167–77.

Goldstein, William. "A Talk with Gloria Naylor." *Publishers' Weekly* 224 (9 Sept. 1983): 35–36.

"Naylor, Gloria." *I Know What the Red Clay Looks Like: The Voice and Vision of Black Women Writers.* Edited by Rebecca Carroll. New York: Crown, 1994, 158–73.

Naylor, Gloria. "Telling Tales and Mississippi Sunsets." *Grand Mothers: Poems, Reminiscences, and Short Stories about the Keepers of Our Traditions.* Edited by Nikki Giovanni. New York: Henry Holt, 1994, 59–62.

——— and Toni Morrison. "A Conversation." *Southern Review* 21 (July 1985): 567–93.

Pate, Willard, ed. "Do You Think of Yourself as a Woman Writer?" *Furman Studies* 34 (Dec. 1988): 2–13.

Pearlman, Mickey. "An Interview with Gloria Naylor." *High Plains Literary Review* 5 (Spring 1990): 98–107.

Pearlman, Mickey, and Katherine Usher Henderson. "Gloria Naylor." *Inter/View: Talks with America's Writing Women.* Lexington: University Press of Kentucky, 1990, 23–29.

Perry, Donna, ed. "Gloria Naylor." *Backtalk: Women Writers Speak Out.* New Brunswick, NJ: Rutgers University Press, 1993, 215–44.

Trescott, Jacqueline. "The Painful Salvation of Gloria Naylor." *Washington Post* 21 Oct. 1983: D1, 4.

"The Woman behind *The Women of Brewster Place.*" *Ebony* 44 (Mar. 1989): 126.

"The Women of Brewster Place." *Ebony* 44 (Mar. 1989): 122–24.

## Selected Contemporary Reviews

### *The Women of Brewster Place*

Glicksman, Marlaine. "Black Like Who?" *Film Comment* 25 (May/June 1989): 75–76. (Television movie review. )

Gottlieb, Annie. "Women Together." *New York Times Book Review* 22 Aug. 1982: 11, 25.

Hairston, Loyle. "A Good First Shot." *Freedomways* 23 (Fourth Quarter 1983): 282–85.

Kendrick, Gerald D. Review. *Journal of Black Studies* 14 (Mar. 1984): 389–90.

*Library Journal* 107 (15 June 1982): 1242.

"Naylor's Fluent, Stark Novel," *Christian Science Monitor* 12 Aug. 1983: B4.

Wickenden, Dorothy. Review. *New Republic* 187 (6 Sept. 1982): 37–38.

### *Linden Hills*

Brown, Joseph A. "With Eyes like Flames of Fire." *Callaloo* 8 (Spring–Summer 1985): 484–88.

Cornish, Sam. "Middle-Class Souls on Ice." *Christian Science Monitor* 1 Mar. 1985: B1.

Gomez, Jewelle. "Naylor's Inferno." *Women's Review of Books* 2 (Aug. 1985): 7–8.

Johnson, Joe. Review. *The Crisis* 92 (May 1985): 13, 47–48.

Jones, Robert. "A Place in the Suburbs." *Commonweal* 112 (3 May 1985): 283–85.

Kaveney, Roz. "Solutions to Dissolution." *TLS* 24 May 1985: 572.

Watkins, Mel. "The Circular Driveways of Hell." *New York Times Book Review* 3 Mar. 1985: 11.

Williams, Sherley Anne. "Roots of Privilege: New Black Fiction." *Ms.* 13 (June 1985): 69–71.


## *Mama Day*

"Book Marks: Summer." *Essence* 19 (July 1988): 28.

Brown, Rosellen. Review. *Ms.* 16 (Feb. 1988): 74.

Hull, Laurence. Review. *Library Journal* 113 (15 Feb. 1988): 179.

*Kirkus Review* 55 (15 Dec. 1987): 1695.

Manuel, Diane. "Return of the Hopeful—Not Happy—Ending." *Christian Science Monitor* 5 Feb. 1988: B1–2.

Mukherjee, Bharati. "There Are Four Sides to Everything." *New York Times Book Review* 21 Feb. 1988: 7.

Newson, Adele S. Review. *SAGE* 6 (Fall 1989): 56–57.

Olson, Patricia. "Gloria Naylor's Unrealized Myth." *Christian Century* 105 (16 Nov. 1988): 1047–48.

Pullin, Faith. "Acts of Reclamation." *TLS* 3–9 June 1988: 623.

Southgate, Martha. "Love's Labors." *Village Voice* 33 (15 Mar. 1988): 52.


## *Bailey's Café*

Brantley, Ben. "A Gathering Place for Hope and Despair." *New York Times* 14 Apr. 1994: C17. (Play review.)

"*Ebony* Book Shelf." *Ebony* 48 (Dec. 1992): 18.

# BIBLIOGRAPHY

Jackson, Thomas. "Review of *Bailey's Café*." *America* 13 Feb. 1993: 17–18.

Jones, Marie. Review. *Library Journal* 117 (1 Sept. 1992): 215.

Kaveney, Roz. "At the Magic Diner." *TLS* 17 July 1992: 20.

Montgomery, Maxine Lavon. Review. *Obsidian II* 8 (Spring–Summer 1993): 111–15.

Taylor, Markland. Review. *Variety* 354 (11 Apr. 1994): 163. (Play review.)

Wakefield, Dan. "Nobody Comes in Here with a Simple Story." *New York Times Book Review* 4 Oct. 1992: 11–12.

Wilentz, Gay. "Healing the Wounds of Time." *Women's Review of Books* 10 (Feb. 1993): 15–16.


## *The Men of Brewster Place*

Hoffman, Roy. "Everyone Deserves a Second Chance." *New York Times Book Review* 19 April 1998:19.

Mundow, Anna. "So Poor, They Didn't Notice When the Great Depression Hit." *Denver Post* 26 April 1998: E4.


# Books about Gloria Naylor

Felton, Sharon, and Michelle C. Loris, eds. *The Critical Response to Gloria Naylor.* Westport, Conn.: Greenwood Press, 1997. Critical essays on the first four novels and interview.

Fowler, Virginia C. *Gloria Naylor: In Search of Sanctuary.* New York: Twayne, 1996. The first close reading of Naylor's fiction; includes chronology and interview.

Gates, Henry Louis, Jr. , and K. A. Appiah, eds. *Gloria Naylor: Critical Perspectives Past and Present.* New York: Amistad, 1993. Critical essays and book reviews.

BIBLIOGRAPHY

# Selected Critical Articles on Gloria Naylor

Andrews, Larry R. "Black Sisterhood in Gloria Naylor's Novels." *CLA Journal* 33 (Sept. 1989): 1–25. Traces the historical depth of the female bond through first three novels, showing movement from early naturalistic to later symbolic and mythical modes.

Awkward, Michael. "Authorial Dreams of Wholeness: (Dis)Unity, (Literary) Parentage, and *The Women of Brewster Place.*" *Inspiriting Influences: Tradition, Revision and Afro-American Women's Novels.* New York: Columbia University Press, 1989, 97–134. Sees Naylor's effort at "redemptive possibilities of female coalescence." Uses Morrison's *Bluest Eye* as point of departure.

Bande, Usha. "Murder as Social Revenge in *The Street* and *The Women of Brewster Place.*" *Notes on Contemporary Literature* 23 (Jan. 1993): 4–5. Looks at differences in the murders in these texts as a strong reaction of women to an unjust social order.

Bobo, Jacqueline, and Ellen Seiter. "Black Feminism and Media Criticism: *The Women of Brewster Place.*" *Screen* 32 (Autumn 1991): 286–302. Analysis of the television version within the "politics of popular cultural representations."

Boyd, Nellie. "Dominion and Proprietorship in Gloria Naylor's *Mama Day* and *Linden Hills.*" *MAWA Review* 5 (Dec. 1990): 56–58. Examination of the leadership methods of Miranda Day and Luther Nedeed and their influence on the other characters.

Christian, Barbara. "Gloria Naylor's Geography: Community, Class, and Patriarchy in *The Women of Brewster Place* and *Linden Hills.*" *Reading Black, Reading Feminist: A Critical Anthology.* Edited by Henry Louis Gates, Jr. New York: Penguin, 1990, 348–73. A look at Naylor's two distinctly different African-American neighborhoods that border on each other.

Christol, Helene. "Reconstructing American History: Land and Genealogy in Gloria Naylor's *Mama Day.*" *The Black Columbiad: Defining Moments in African American Literature and Culture.*

Edited by Werner Sollors and Maria Diedrich. Cambridge: Harvard University Press, 1994, 347–56. Argues that Naylor develops a "parallel black history" by undermining the dominant "historical and mythical elements."

Collins, G. Michelle. "There Where We Are Not: The Magical Real in *Beloved* and *Mama Day*." *Southern Review* 24 (Summer 1988): 680–85. Collins explains how these novels use magical realism to expand the reader's consciousness of reality.

Donlon, Jocelyn Hazelwood. "Hearing is Believing: Southern Racial Communities and Strategies of Story-Listening in Gloria Naylor and Lee Smith." *Twentieth Century Literature* 41 (Spring 1995): 16–35. In *Mama Day* and *Oral History,* Donlon suggests the authors do not trust the American reader to hear stories told differently.

Eckard, Paula Gallant. "The Prismatic Past in *Oral History* and *Mama Day*." *MELUS* 20 (Fall 1995): 121–36. Eckard examines in the novels of Lee Smith and Naylor their deconstruction and re-examination of the past in these two different Southern settings.

Eko, Ebele. "Beyond the Myth of Confrontation: A Comparative Study of African and African-American Female Protagonists." *Ariel* 17 (Oct. 1986): 139–52. Among other examples, Eko uses Kiswana Browne of *Brewster Place* to demonstrate how women are determined "to stand for equity and choice."

Fraser, Celeste. "Stealing B(l)ack Voices: The Myth of the Black Matriarchy and *The Women of Brewster Place*." *Critical Matrix* 5 (Fall–Winter 1989): 65–88. Naylor's images of black women measured against the political fictions of the Moynihan Report, a 1964 document which posited a negative stereotype of black families.

Gates, Henry Louis, Jr. "Significant Others." *Contemporary Literature* 29 (1988): 606–23. Concerning *Linden Hills,* Gates challenges Homans' choice of using Irigaray's article as appropriate, for he sees a homoerotic attraction between Willie and Lester and from Luther to Willie, a topic which Irigaray's work does not address.

Harris, Trudier. "The Eye as Voice and Ear: African Southern Orality and Folklore in Gloria Naylor's *Mama Day*." *The Power of the Porch: The Storyteller's Craft in Zora Neale Hurston, Gloria Naylor, and Randall Kenan.* Athens: University of Georgia Press, 1996, 53–104. Harris explores how Naylor reclaims the South, building on the expectations of an African-American audience familiar with a combination of the supernatural, storytelling, and folklore.

Homans, Margaret. "The Woman in the Cave: Recent Feminist Fictions and the Classical Underworld." *Contemporary Literature* 29 (1988): 369–402. A feminist reading of *Linden Hills* beside Luce Irigaray's *Speculum of the Other.* Homans suggests Naylor tells a story not told by Plato, "the story of a woman in a cave."

Kelley, Margot Anne. "Sisters' Choices: Quilting Aesthetics in Contemporary African American Women's Fiction." *Quilt Culture: Tracing the Pattern.* Edited by Cheryl B. Torsney and Judy Elsley. Columbia: University of Missouri Press, 1994, 49–67. Explores the African-American quilting aesthetic in *Mama Day,* showing how Cocoa is constructed from all the people who are represented in the double-ring wedding quilt.

Korenman, Joan S. "African-American Women Writers, Black Nationalism, and the Matrilineal Heritage." *CLA Journal* 38 (Dec. 1994): 143–61. Looks at Walker's "Everyday Use," Bambara's "My Man Bovanne," and Naylor's Kiswana Browne in *The Women of Brewster Place,* examining how daughters who are discovering their ties to Africa and Black nationalism sit in judgment of their "politically incorrect" mothers.

Kubitschek, Missy Dehn. "Toward a New Order: Shakespeare, Morrison, and Gloria Naylor's *Mama Day*." *MELUS: The Journal for the Study of the Multi-Ethnic Literature of the United States* 19 (Fall 1994): 75–90. Arguing that Naylor's novel defies interpretation through an exclusive Euro-American view because of the

# BIBLIOGRAPHY

"past's persistence in the present, the present's participation in myth and archetype," Kubitschek initiates an exploration of the allusions in the text.

Lee, Valerie. "Conjure Discourse in Conjuring Communities: *Mama Day* and Fieldwork in Paradise." *Granny Midwives and Black Women Writers: Double-Dutched Readings.* New York: Routledge, 1996, 129–69. Explores *Mama Day* as example of a whole community of conjurers, who deal in midwifery, rootworking, and healing skills, and places Dr. Buzzard within an historical and legendary tradition of folk medicine tales. Juxtaposed by Lee's fieldwork in Mississippi and interviews with midwives.

Levy, Helen Fiddyment. "Lead on with Light: Gloria Naylor." *Fiction of the Home Place.* Jackson: University Press of Mississippi, 1992, 196–222. Looks at Naylor's version of the home beside images from the fiction of Jewett, Cather, Glasgow, Porter, and Welty.

Lynch, Michael F. "The Wall and the Mirror in the Promised Land: The City in the Novels of Gloria Naylor." *The City in African-American Literature.* Madison: Fairleigh Dickinson University Press, 1995, 181–95. In Naylor's first three novels, Lynch sees Naylor following in the line of other African-American writers who also reject the "romantic quest for an Eden"; in addition, Naylor's characters go inside themselves to search for ways to transform the places in which they live.

Meisenhelder, Susan. "'Eating Cane' in Gloria Naylor's *The Women of Brewster Place* and Zora Neale Hurston's 'Sweat.'" *Notes on Contemporary Literature* 23 (Mar. 1993): 5–7. Meisenhelder makes a connection between Butch Fuller's eating cane and a similar position expressed in Hurston's "Sweat."

———. "'The Whole Picture' in Gloria Naylor's *Mama Day*." *African American Review* 27 (Fall 1993): 405–19. Meisenhelder argues that Naylor's novel is a demonstration of the complexity of black cultural identity that refuses the control of a white world.

# BIBLIOGRAPHY

Montgomery, Maxine L. "The Fathomless Dream: Gloria Naylor's Use of the Descent Motif in *The Women of Brewster Place*." *CLA Journal* 36 (Sept. 1992): 1–11. Suggests that Naylor documents the "failure of the American dream" and questions its validity.

———. "Authority, Multivocality, and the New World Order in Gloria Naylor's *Bailey's Café*." *African American Review* 29 (Spring 1995): 27–33. A reading of the novel that highlights Naylor's use of biblical stories to reclaim and see anew women's assigned place in a male-authored text.

Palumbo, Kathryn. "The Uses of Female Imagery in Naylor's *The Women of Brewster Place*." *Notes on Contemporary Literature* 15 (May 1985): 6–7. Calls attention to female imagery, particularly the use of the color red, to show heroic behavior of women.

Puhr, Kathleen M. "Healers in Gloria Naylor's Fiction." *Twentieth Century Literature* 40 (Winter 1994): 518–27. Explores the ways Naylor uses various healing methods in her novels—holistic, archetypal, and links to African rituals.

Sandiford, K. A. "Gothic and Intertextual Constructions in *Linden Hills*." *Arizona Quarterly* 47 (Autumn 1991): 117–39. Examines the multivoiced discourse within the novel that highlights its gothic elements.

Saunders, James Robert. "The Ornamentation of Old Ideas: Gloria Naylor's First Three Novels." *Hollins Critic* 27 (Apr. 1990): 1–11. Makes connections between *Brewster Place* and Petry's *The Street; Linden Hills* and *The Inferno*; *Mama Day* and *Hamlet* and *The Tempest*.

———. "From the Hypocrisy of the Reverend Woods to Mama Day's Faith of the Spirit." *The Wayward Preacher in the Literature of African American Women*. Jefferson, NC: McFarland & Co., 1995, 105–24. Suggests that Naylor makes a case for women's spirituality flourishing best in a space without men.

Storhoff, Gary. "'The Only Voice Is Your Own': Gloria Naylor's

# BIBLIOGRAPHY

Revision of *The Tempest.*" *African American Review* 29 (Spring 1995): 35–45. Looks at how Naylor claims her own voice in reshaping *The Tempest,* supplanting Prospero who would not accept backtalk with a Miranda who serves as guide to the island. Helpful comments on Naylor's use of eggs as "trope for Miranda's way of life."

Tanner, Laura E. "Reading Rape: *Sanctuary* and *The Women of Brewster Place.*" *American Literature* 62 (Dec. 1990): 559–82. Argues that in Naylor's rape scene the victim is not an "erotic object," but that the reader's gaze is directed at the violator.

Tingley, Stephanie A. "'A Ring of Pale Women': Willa Nedeed as Feminist Archivist and Historian in Gloria Naylor's *Linden Hills.*" *Critic* 57 (Winter 1995): 59–67. Explores Willa's "journey toward self-discovery" as an examination of African-American women's history.

Toombs, Charles P. "The Confluence of Food and Identity in Gloria Naylor's *Linden Hills:* What We Eat is Who We Is.'" *CLA Journal* 37 (Sept. 1993): 1–18. How a healthy African-American identity is linked to food consumption, and in the novel the food choices help dismantle the well-being of the individuals in this community.

Traub, Valerie. "Rainbows of Darkness: Deconstructing Shakespeare in the Work of Gloria Naylor and Zora Neale Hurston." *Cross-Cultural Performances: Differences in Women's Re-Visions of Shakespeare.* Edited by Marianne Novy. Urbana: Universityof Illinois Press, 1993,150–64. Explores Naylor's use of invoking and distancing Shakespeare in *Mama Day.*

Tucker, Lindsey. "Recovering the Conjure Woman: Texts and Contexts in Gloria Naylor's *Mama Day.*" *African American Review* 28 (Summer 1994): 173–88. Tucker argues that Naylor's use of multiple conjurers relies on a tradition that demands a different narrative mode and an altered response from readers.

# BIBLIOGRAPHY

Wagner-Martin, Linda. "Quilting in Gloria Naylor's *Mama Day*." *Notes on Contemporary Literature* 18 (Nov. 1988): 6–7. Looking at Mama Day's work on the double-ring quilt, Wagner-Martin connects the quilting activity with the strong bond that affects women, one generation to another.

Wallinger, Hanna. "Gloria Naylor's *Linden Hills:* The Novel by an African American Woman Writer and the Critical Discourse." *Moderne Sprachen* 37 (1993): 172–86. A response, in part, to Homans, Gates, Ward, and Sandiford, who represent various schools of critical thought. Wallinger adds that Naylor, in places, leans on the African side of her heritage in the use of spatial configurations and ant imagery.

Ward, Catherine C. "Gloria Naylor's *Linden Hills:* A Modern Inferno." *Contemporary Literature* 28 (1987): 67–81. A close and detailed allegorical reading of Naylor's use of Dante's work in her novel.

Warren, Nagueyalti. "Cocoa and George: A Love Dialectic." *SAGE* 7 (Fall 1990): 19–25. Warren contrasts the feeling of Cocoa with the logical thought of George in an exploration of how the couple's love relationship moves from the erotic to the spiritual plane.

Wells, Linda. "'What Shall I Give My Children?' The Role of the Mentor in Gloria Naylor's *The Women of Brewster Place* and Paule Marshall's *Praisesong for the Widow.*" *Explorations in Ethnic Studies* 13 (July 1990): 41–60. In a marginalized society, the effects of strong mentoring are essential to a community's sense of worth.

# INDEX